The Old Vic and Wise Children present

WISE CHILDREN
by Angela Carter

Adapted and directed by Emma Rice

Co-produced by Belgrade Theatre Coventry,
Oxford Playhouse and York Theatre Royal

Wise Children is a new theatre company created and led by Emma Rice. It is the beginning of a new chapter, and the culmination of the practice and ethos Emma has developed over her unique 30 year career. From our base in the South West, we will create landmark work with exceptional artists, challenge outmoded touring models, train the next generation of creative practitioners through Emma Rice's School for Wise Children and discover the creative spaces of the future.

Wise Children's first public performance, which was also the first performance of this production, took place at The Old Vic, London, on 6 October 2018.

Wise Children is supported by Arts Council England as a National Portfolio Organisation and the production is made possible by the generous support of The Broughton Family Charitable Trust, The London Community Foundation, and Cockayne Grants for the Arts.

Wise Children is a Resident Company at The Old Vic and an Associate at Bristol Old Vic.

CAST

Young Peregrine
Sam Archer

Young Melchior
Ankur Bahl

Showgirl Nora
Omari Douglas

Young Nora
Mirabelle Gremaud

Melchior
Paul Hunter

Showgirl Dora
Melissa James

Young Dora
Bettrys Jones

Wheelchair/Lady Atalanta
/Blue Eyed Boy
Patrycja Kujawska

Nora Chance
Etta Murfitt

Grandma Chance
Katy Owen

Peregrine
Mike Shepherd

Dora Chance
Gareth Snook

Musicians
Stu Barker
Alex Heane
Ian Ross

ARTISTIC TEAM

Director
Emma Rice

Set & Costume Designer
Vicki Mortimer

Composer & Musical Director
Ian Ross

Lighting Design
Malcolm Rippeth

Sound & Video Design
Simon Baker

Choreography
Etta Murfitt

Animation
Beth Carter
& Stuart Mitchell

Puppetry Design
Lyndie Wright

Puppetry Director
Sarah Wright

Fights
Rachel Bown-Williams
Ruth Cooper-Brown

Associate Sound
Jay Jones

Assistant Choreography
Tom Jackson Greaves

Assistant Director
Balisha Karra

PRODUCTION TEAM

Props Supervisor
Lizzie Frankl

Costume Supervisor
Lucy Martin

Casting
Sam Jones CDG

Voice Coach
Jonathan Dawes

Production Manager
Cath Bates

Company Stage Manager
Steph Curtis

Assistant Stage Manager
Charlie Smalley

Rehearsal Stage Manager
Laura Deards

Touring Stage Manager
Aled Thomas

Head of Sound
Charlie Simpson

Sound No 2
Angela Gomez

Production Sound Engineers
Sam Palmer
Adam Washington

Production Video Engineer
Beth Thompson

Lighting Programmer
Will Ferris

Production Electrician
Laurence Russell

Touring LX
Joe Crossley

Head of Wardrobe and Wigs
Ryan Walklett

Deputy Wardrobe and Wigs
Rachael Nevill

WISE CHILDREN

Artistic Director
Emma Rice

Movement Director
Etta Murfitt

Executive Director
Judith Dimant

Finance Manager
Delyth Thompson

Executive Producer
Poppy Keeling

Acting Assistant Producer
Ginny Graham

Director of Music
Ian Ross

Administrator
Matt Lister

Digital Associate
Simon Baker

Thanks

Artspace Lifespace, Becki Boot, Alan Brodie, Guiseppe Cannas, Susannah Clapp, Rob Connick, Ryan O'Conner, Ros Coombes, Eddie Crowther, Heather Cryan, Eleanor Dolan, Lottie Donovan, Damon Edwards, Molly Einchcomb, Miraculous Engineering, Paul Evans, Gabrielle Firth, Kara Fitzpatrick, Shakespeare's Globe, Charles Hanrahan, Amy Hawthorne, Danni Haylett, Matt Hellyer, Phil Hurly, Kerry Jarrett, Natasha Jayatileke, Aislinn Luton, White Light, Ben Marshall, Paul Mathew, Hatley Print, Christina Poulton, Aniqah Rawat, Mein Roberts, Kirsti Reid, Data Reprographics, Lorraine Richards, Will Skeet, Jane Smith, Flora Snelson, Stage Sound Services, Steve Tanner, Sean Teng, Rebekah Wild, Lucy Williams, Lucy Woollatt, Jackie Young, and all members of the Wise Children Club.

CAST

Sam Archer Young Peregrine

Theatre includes: *An Ideal Husband, We Will Rock You, Oliver!, Bugsy Malone* (West End); Chariots of Fire (Hampstead/West End); *Wonder.land* (National Theatre/Châtelet Theatre, Paris); *Earthquakes in London* (National Theatre/UK Tour); *The Soldier's Tale* (Metropolitan Theatre, Tokyo); *La Bohéme* (Royal Albert Hall); *Metamorphosis* (Joyce Theatre, New York); *The Red Shoes, Cinderella, Lord of the Flies, Swan Lake, The Car Man, Play Without Words, Nutcracker, Edward Scissorhands* (Matthew Bourne's New Adventures Company); *Gloriana* (ROH); *The Wind in the Willows* (Linbury Studio Theatre) and *Oklahoma* (Chichester) and *Mary Poppins* (UK Tour).

Television includes: *Humans* and *Mr Selfridge*.

Film includes: *Allied, Muppets Most Wanted* and *Life is a Buffet*.

Ankur Bahl Young Melchior

Theatre includes: *A Midsummer Night's Dream* (Shakespeare's Globe); *This Beach* (Brokentalkers, Ireland); *Volpone, The Empress, The Comedy of Errors, The Tempest, Twelfth Night* (RSC); *Can We Talk About This* (DV8); *Miranda* (Assembly Rooms/Tara Arts); *Britain's Got Bhangra, Where's My Desi Soulmate* (Rifco Arts); *To Be Straight With You* (National Theatre/DV8); *Just Add Water* (Shobana Jeyasingh Dance Company); *Seven Deadly Sins* (Welsh National Opera) and *Shades of Passion* (National Dance Company of Wales).

Film includes: *Voices of Finance, The Surprise, Honeycomb Lodge, Desi Boyz* and *Jump Nation*.

Omari Douglas Showgirl Nora

Theatre includes: *High Society* (The Old Vic); *Five Guys Named Moe, Elegies for Angels, Punks and Raging Queens* (West End); *Rush* (King's Head Theatre); *Peter Pan, Jesus Christ Superstar* (Regent's Park Open Air Theatre); *Tristan and Yseult* (Shakespeare's Globe); *The Life* (Southwark Playhouse); *Annie Get Your Gun* (Sheffield Crucible); *When the Waters Recede* (Theatre by the Lake) and *Hairspray* (Curve, Leicester/UK Tour).

Mirabelle Gremaud Young Nora

Mirabelle has worked with companies including: Acrojou (circus/theatre); Urban Conceptz Theatre (dance/theatre); Georgina Starr (performance artist).

Other work under the name 'Le Mirabellier', includes: a solo dance piece at the Resolution Festival 2018 at The Place, London and the Fun Fatale Festival 2018, Prague. She graduated from the Accademia Teatro Dimitri and has a post-graduate degree from the Laban Conservatory of Dance. Her performance involves elements from circus, acrobatics, contortion and hand-balancing.

Paul Hunter Melchior

Theatre includes: *My Perfect Mind* (Told By An Idiot/Young Vic/New York); *The Play What I Wrote* (West End/Liverpool Playhouse); *The Little Match Girl and Other Happier Tales, The Mystery Plays, Much Ado About Nothing, Troilus and Cressida, A Midsummer Night's Dream, Under the Black Flag* (Shakespeare's Globe); *Napoleon Disrobed, The Farenheit Twins, Don't Laugh — It's My Life, You Haven't Embraced Me Yet, I'm So Big, On The Verge of Exploding* (Told by an Idiot/UK Tour); *Life of Galileo* (Young Vic); *The Water Engine* (Young Vic/Theatre 503); *Rapunzel, The Red Shoes* (Kneehigh) and *Les Enfants Du Paradis* (RSC).

Television includes: *Black Books* and *Marvellous*.

Film includes: *Maleficent, Pirates of the Caribbean, Cinderella* and *Snow White and the Huntsman*.

Melissa James Showgirl Dora

Theatre includes: *Eugenius!* (West End); *The Two Noble Kinsmen* (Shakespeare's Globe); *One Love: The Bob Marley Musical* (Birmingham Rep); *Annie Get Your Gun* (Sheffield Crucible); *A Midsummer Night's Dream* (Theatre Royal Bath); *The Bodyguard, Cats* (UK Tour), *Guys and Dolls* (Chichester) and *West Side Story* (RSC).

Television includes: *Training Days, Ransom, Dead Pixels, Waffle the Wonderdog, Thanks for the Memories, Holby City, Silent Witness, WPC 56* and *Doctors*.

Bettrys Jones Young Dora

Theatre includes: *Wait Until Dark* (West End); *War Horse* (National Theatre/West End); *A Midsummer Night's Dream, Comedy Of Errors* (RSC/West End); *Hamlet, The Little Match Girl and Other Happier Tales, As You Like It* (Shakespeare's Globe); *The Tin Drum* (Kneehigh); *Life Of Galileo* (Young Vic); *We Want You To Watch, Edward II* (National Theatre); *Praxis Makes Perfect* (National Theatre Wales); *Sleeping Beauties* (Sherman Theatre); *The Mouse And His Child* (RSC); *The Snow Queen* (Rose Theatre Kingston); *The Dark Philosophers* (Traverse); *And The Horse You Rode In On* (Drum Theatre/Barbican); *The Crucible* (Regent's Park Open Air Theatre); *Measure For Measure, Cariad* (Theatre Clwyd) and *To Kill A Mockingbird* (Leeds Playhouse/Birmingham Rep).

Patrycja Kujawska Wheelchair/Lady Atlanta/Blue Eyed Boy

Theatre includes: *Drop Dead Gorgeous, Let the Mountains Lead You to Love, Punch Drunk, Broken Chords, Fairy Tale, Test Run, If We Go On, Motherland, Underworld* (Vincent Dance Theatre); *Don John* (Kneehigh/RSC); *Midnight's Pumpkin, The Red Shows, The Wild Bride, Tristan and Yseult, Dead Dog in a Suitcase, 946 The Amazing Story of Adolphus Tips, The Tin Drum* (Kneehigh) and *The Grinning Man* (Bristol Old Vic).

Other work includes: physical theatre with Dada Von Bzdulow and City Theatre in Gdynia. Patrycja studied violin at the Academy of Music, Poland.

Etta Murfitt Nora

Theatre as Choreographer with Emma Rice includes: *The Umbrellas of Cherbourg* (Kneehigh/Leicester Curve/West End); *The Flying Lovers of Vitebsk, 946, The Wild Bride, Midnight's Pumpkin, Steptoe and Son* (Kneehigh); *Twelfth Night* and *A Midsummer Night's Dream* (Shakespeare's Globe).

Other theatre as Choreographer includes: *Dead Dog in a Suitcase* and *Tin Drum* (Kneehigh/UK Tour).

Theatre as an Associate Artistic Director and performer for Matthew Bourne's New Adventures includes: *Sleeping Beauty, Cinderella* (Sadler's Wells/LA); *Dorian Gray, Edward Scissorhands, Nutcracker!* (Opera North/Sadler's Wells); *The Car Man, Swan Lake* and *The Red Shoes* (Sadler's Wells/West End/LA/Broadway).

Etta is an Associate Artist with Kneehigh Theatre Company.

Katy Owen Grandma Chance

Theatre includes: *UBU-Karaoke* (Kneehigh); *Twelfth Night, A Midsummer Night's Dream (Shakespeare's Globe); The Little Matchgirl and Other Happier Tales* (Bristol Old Vic/Shakespeare's Globe/UK Tour); *946 The Amazing Story of Adolphus Tips* (Kneehigh/Shakespeare's Globe/UK Tour/ USA Tour); *Rebecca* (Kneehigh); *The World of Work, The Night Before Christmas* (Chapter Arts Centre); *Apparitions of Spirits with the Forsythe Sisters* (Gaggle Babble); *Maudie's Rooms, Plum — And Me, Will, Cinders* (Sherman Theatre); *The Little Matchgirl* and *The Tempest* (Theatr Iolo).

Film includes: *Daddy's Girl.*

Television includes: *Casualty* and *The Story of Tracy Beaker.*

Mike Shepherd Peregrine

Theatre as Director includes: *Dead Dog in a Suitcase (and other love songs)* (Kneehigh/European Tour); *A Very Old Man with Enormous Wings* (Little Angel) and *The Tin Drum* (Kneehigh).

Theatre as Performer includes: *Tristan & Yseult, Steptoe and Son, Midnight's Pumpkin, The Red Shoes, The Bacchae, Cymbeline, The Wooden Frock, A Matter of Life and Death, Don John* and *Ubu-Karaoke* (Kneehigh).

Film includes: *Anna Karenina* and *Pan.*

Mike is the Artistic Director of Kneehigh Theatre and works with the Paraorchestra and Good Chance Theatre.

Gareth Snook Dora

Theatre includes: *Phantom of the Opera, My Fair Lady, Aspects of Love, Sunset Boulevard, The Rink, Les Miserables, The Hired Man, Guys and Dolls, Cats, Girlfriends, Closer Than Ever, Made in Dagenham, Hey, Mr Producer* (West End); *Assassins, Company* (Donmar/West End); *Romantics Anonymous, Romeo & Juliet* (Shakespeare's Globe); *Fiddler on the Roof* (Chichester); *A Pacifist's Guide to the War on Cancer* (National Theatre); *Casa Valentina* (Southwark Playhouse); *Show Boat* (Royal Albert Hall); *The Full Monty* and *Martin Guerre* (UK Tour).

Television includes: *Taboo, Law & Order: UK, Emmerdale* and *French & Saunders.*

Film includes: *Les Miserables* and *Paddington 2.*

BAND
Stu Barker

Theatre as Composer/Musical Director includes: *Brief Encounter* (Broadway/West End); *A Matter Of Life And Death, Tristan And Yseult* (National Theatre); *Cymbeline, Don John, The Empress* (RSC); *A Midsummer Night's Dream, A Winter's Tale, Romeo And Juliet* (Shakespeare's Globe); *946 The Amazing Story of Adolphus Tips* (Kneehigh); *Hansel And Gretel* (Bristol Old Vic); *The Bacchae, The Wooden Frock* (Leeds Playhouse); *Nights At The Circus, The Red Shoes* (Lyric Hammersmith); *The Wild Bride, Rapunzel, Midnight Pumpkin* (BAC) and *Pandora's Box* (Northern Stage).

Other theatre includes: *The Grinning Man* (West End).

Television includes: *The Cult Of The Suicide Bomber* and *Beyond Grief.*

Radio includes: *Tracks.*

Alex Heane

Theatre includes: *Hetty Feather* (Rose Theatre Kingston/West End); *The Tallest Horse on Earth* (Silly Boys Theatre); *Jane Eyre* (National Theatre); *The Little Matchgirl and Other Happier Tales* (Shakespeare's Globe); *Cinderella: A Fairytale* (Travelling Light/Tobacco Factory Theatres) and *100: The Day Our World Changed* (Wildworks Theatre).

Alex is a musician with the band Branwelland With Flares.

Ian Ross

Theatre as Performer and Music Director for Kneehigh includes: *The Red Shoes*, *Don John*, *The Wild Bride*, *Tristan and Yseult*, *Dead Dog in a Suitcase* and *The Flying Lovers of Vitebsk*.

Theatre as Composer includes: *Twelfth Night* (Shakespeare's Globe); *The Very Old Man with Enormous Wings* and *The Flying Lovers of Vitebsk* (Kneehigh).

Ian is an Associate Artist of Kneehigh and Director of Music for Wise Children.

CREATIVE TEAM

Emma Rice Adaptation/Director

Theatre includes: *Romantics Anonymous, Twelfth Night, A Midsummer Night's Dream, The Little Matchgirl and Other Happier Tales* (Shakespeare's Globe); *The Flying Lovers of Vitebsk, Tristan & Yseult, 946 The Amazing Story of Adolphus Tips, The Wild Bride, The Red Shoes, The Wooden Frock, The Bacchae, Cymbeline, A Matter of Life and Death, Rapunzel, Brief Encounter, Don John, Wah! Wah! Girls, Steptoe and Son* (Kneehigh); *Oedipussy* (UK Tour); *The Empress* (RSC); *The Umbrellas of Cherbourg* (West End) and *An Audience with Meow Meow* (Berkeley Repertory Theatre).

Emma has been Artistic Director at Shakespeare's Globe and Kneehigh and is now Artistic Director of her new company, Wise Children.

Vicki Mortimer Set & Costume Design

Theatre includes: *Follies* — Critics' Circle Award for Design, Olivier Award for Best Costume Design, *The Plough and the Stars, The Threepenny Opera, Here We Go, The Silver Tassie, Othello, Hamlet, Waves, Cat in the Hat, Three Sisters, The Seagull, Closer, Paul, The Last of the Haussmans* (National Theatre) and work for other companies including: Kneehigh, Young Vic, Royal Court, Chichester, RSC and Almeida.

Opera design for companies includes: ROH, Glyndebourne, Aix and Salzburg Festivals, ENO.

Ballet design includes new works by Wayne McGregor, and the Royal Ballet.

Malcolm Rippeth Lighting

Theatre and opera includes: *Brief Encounter* — WhatsOnStage Award for Best Lighting Designer, Village Voice OBIE Award for Design, *The Umbrellas of Cherbourg, Calendar Girls, Six Characters in Search of an Author* (West End); *Romantics Anonymous, Twelfth Night* (Shakespeare's Globe); *The Flying Lovers of Vitebsk, The Tin Drum, Tristan & Yseult* (Kneehigh); *Titus Andronicus* (RSC); *Decade* (Headlong); *The Boy in the Striped*

Pyjamas (Chichester); *The Dead* (Abbey Dublin); *The Birthday Party* (Royal Exchange, Manchester); *Spur of the Moment* (Royal Court); *My Brilliant Friend* (Rose Theatre Kingston); *Pleasure* (Opera North); *The Skating Rink* (Garsington Opera); *War & Peace* (Welsh National Opera) and *Alcina* (Santa Fe Opera).

Simon Baker Sound & Video Design
Theatre includes: *A Christmas Carol, The Caretaker, The Master Builder, Future Conditional, High Society, Electra, The Norman Conquests, Hedda Gabler, The Real Thing* (The Old Vic); *Girl from the North Country; Groundhog Day* (The Old Vic/Broadway); *The Moderate Soprano, Shakespeare in Love, Mojo* (West End); *Matilda The Musical* — Olivier Award for Best Sound (RSC/West End/Broadway/UK Tour); *Twelfth Night, A Midsummer Night's Dream* (Shakespeare's Globe); *Pinocchio, The Light Princess, Amen Corner* (National Theatre); *The Roaring Girl* (RSC); *The Grinning Man* (Bristol Old Vic/West End); *Tristan & Yseult, Brief Encounter, The Red Shoes, The Wild Bride, Don John, Steptoe & Son, 946: The Amazing Story of Adolphus Tips, Rebecca* and *The Flying Lovers* (Kneehigh).

Ian Ross Composer
See the Cast page for full biography.

Etta Murfitt Choreographer
See the Cast page for full biography.

Beth Carter & Stuart Mitchell Animation
Beth is a visual artist, working in sculpture, drawing and print. Her figurative work is displayed in galleries in the UK, Belgium and the US and held in international collections. Stuart is an interdisciplinary artist, experimenting with digital technology, painting and print. He has worked with public arts commissioners, art galleries, film and animation festivals, visual artists, musicians and choreographers and his work has been shown in galleries and at art fairs both in the UK and internationally. Beth and Stuart have collaborated to work on animation in recent years.

Lyndie Wright Puppetry Design

Lyndie has worked for companies including: Kneehigh, RSC, The Globe, Opera North, Puppet Players, Silent Tide, Little Angel Theatre, and created international puppet collections. She and her husband, John Wright, founded Little Angel Theatre in 1961.

Sarah Wright Puppetry Director

Theatre as Puppet Director includes: *Nice Fish* (West End); *Dancing Frog, The Tin Drum, Dead Dog in a Suitcase (and Other Love Songs)*; *946 The Amazing Story of Adolphus Tips, Brief Encounter, Red Shoes* (Kneehigh); *Life of Galileo, A Season in the Congo* (Young Vic); *The Little Match Girl* (Shakespeare's Globe); *Angelo* (Little Angel); *Silent Tide, Adventures of Curious Ganz* (Silent Tide) and *Sleeping Beauty* (Matthew Bourne's New Adventures).

Theatre as Performer includes: *The Tin Drum, Dead Dog in a Suitcase* (Kneehigh); *Venus and Adonis* (RSC) and *A Very Old Man with Enormous Wings* (Little Angel). Sarah is Artistic Director of the Curious School of Puppetry and Associate Artist at Kneehigh and Little Angel Theatre.

Rachel Bown-Williams & Ruth Cooper-Brown of R-C Annie Ltd Fights

Theatre includes: *A Monster Calls, Woyzeck* (The Old Vic); *The Little Matchgirl* (Bristol Old Vic/Shakespeare's Globe); *Emilia, Othello, The Secret Theatre, Boudica, Lions and Tigers, Much Ado About Nothing; Twelfth Night, The White Devil, Comus and Imogen* (Shakespeare's Globe); *Tartuffe, The Duchess of Malfi, Salome, Snow in Midsummer* (RSC); *God of Carnage, The Price, Switzerland, Dusty* (Theatre Royal Bath); *The Village* (Theatre Royal Stratford East); *Girl on a Train, Sunshine on Leith, The Lion, The Witch and The Wardrobe, Barnbow Canaries, Great Expectations, Richard III* (Leeds Playhouse); *A Clockwork Orange* (Liverpool Everyman); *Common, Ugly Lies the Bone, Peter Pan, The Threepenny Opera, The James Plays* and *Cleansed* (National Theatre).

Lizzie Frankl Props Supervisor

Theatre includes: *An Ideal Husband, The Exorcist, Cat on a Hot Tin Roof, Don Juan in Soho, Nice Fish, Mojo, Wind in the Willows, Aladdin, Funny Girl, A Christmas Carol* (West End); *Dynamo and Derren Brown* (UK tours); *Blithe Spirit* (Ahmanson, Los Angeles); *The River* (Circle in the Square, New York); *Monty Python Live* (O2 Arena) and *The Testament of Mary* (Walter Kerr, New York).

Other theatre includes productions for: The Old Vic, Donmar Warehouse, Chichester Festival Theatre, Theatre Royal Bath and ENO. Lizzie Props Ltd also provided the props for Stormzy at the Brit Awards 2018, Mariah Carey's Christmas Tour and Robbie Williams' world Tour.

Lucy Martin Costume Supervisor

Theatre as Costume Supervisor includes: *Woyzeck* (The Old Vic); *Red Velvet* (West End); *Summer and Smoke* (Almeida/ West End); *Little Shop Of Horrors* (Regent's Park Open Air Theatre); *Romantics Anonymous, Boudica, The Little Match Girl* (Shakespeare's Globe); *Cosi Fan Tutti* (Central City Opera, Colorado); *Dry Powder, IHO or The Intelligent Homosexuals Guide To Capitalism, Socialism with a Key to The Scriptures* (Hampstead); *Absolute Hell, Julie, The Deep Blue Sea* (National Theatre); *Elegy, The Vote* (Donmar); *Macbeth, La Musica, Creditors, The Cherry Orchard* (Young Vic); *Crouch, Touch, Pause, Engage* (National Theatre Wales/Out of Joint) *Mametz* (National Theatre Wales); *IGNIS* (Print Room); *Dedication, The Nutcracker* (Nuffield Theatre) and *The Master and Margarita* (Complicité/Barbican/European Tour).

Balisha Karra Baylis Assistant Director

Theatre as Assistant Director includes: *How to Spot an Alien; Island Town, Sticks and Stones* (Paines Plough); *Present Laughter* (Chichester) and *Freeman* (Strictly Arts UK Tour).

Theatre as Trainee Assistant Director includes: *A Midsummer Night's Dream* (Young Vic).

Balisha has held positions as Resident Trainee Director at Paines Plough and Resident Director at Birmingham Repertory Theatre's Foundry. She is the current Baylis Assistant Director at The Old Vic and recipient of the Florence Kleiner Bursary.

Jay Jones Associate Sound Designer

Theatre as Sound Designer includes: *OV200 Gala* (The Old Vic); *Gate Gala* (St Paul's, Hammersmith) and *Plastic* (Ustinov Studio, Bath).

Theatre as Associate Designer includes: *A Christmas Carol* (The Old Vic); *Girl from the North Country* (The Old Vic/West End); *The Grinning Man* (West End); *Brief Encounter* (Empire Cinema Haymarket); *The Little Match Girl and Other Happier Tales*(Bristol Old Vic/Shakespeare's Globe/UK Tour); *Tristan & Yseult* (Kneehigh/UK Tour); *Dead Dog in a Suitcase* (Kneehigh/World Tour) and *946* (Kneehigh/Asylum/World Tour).

Jay worked as Head of Sound at Shakespeare's Globe for two years under the artistic leadership of Emma Rice.

Tom Jackson Greaves Assistant Choreographer

Theatre as Director includes: *Run For Your Life* (Kneehigh); *Neptunalia* (Cscape); *Seven Deadly Sins* (UK Tour) and *Vanity Fowl* (Sadler's Wells).

Theatre as Choreographer/Movement Director include: *The Dancing Frog* (Kneehigh); Sweet Charity, The Borrowers, Frankenstein, A Midsummer Night's Dream, Twelfth Night, Romeo and Juliet (The Watermill); *Paint Your Wagon, Fiddler On The Roof* (Liverpool Everyman); *Teddy* (UK Tour); *Boudica, The Two Gentlemen of Verona* (Shakespeare's Globe); The Glass Menagerie (Headlong); Spring Awakening (Hope Mill Manchester); *The Life* (Southwark Playhouse); Peter and the Starcatcher (Northampton Royal & Derngate) and *The Crocodile* (Manchester International Festival).

Tom received the New Adventures Choreographer Award in 2012 and is an associate artist at The Watermill.

Thank you!

It has taken an army of friends and colleagues to help me turn Wise Children from dream to reality and I am forever in their debt! Thank you to my Creative Cabinet at Shakespeare's Globe and my temporary team of advisors for Wise Children including David Jubb, Mike Shepherd, Tanika Gupta, Gisli Orn Gardarsson, Vicki Mortimer, Clare Reddington and Sally O'Neill. A heartful of gratitude and affection goes to Monica Bakir, Matthew Dunster and my theatre team at The Globe who lived through such turbulence with consistent generosity, loyalty and fun. Lifelong love and gratitude goes to Kneehigh who have remained my supportive family always, and solidarity and respect goes to my technical teams at The Globe who stood by me on the way in – and on the way out. Cheers also to my new team at Wise children who have taught me again what a joy it is to dance and sing!

My biggest thanks go to two people without whom I couldn't have kept going, let alone thrive. Allegra Galvin and Simon Baker. Boundless love, endless butterflies and loud cheers for my treasured and original Wise Children.

Emma Rice

Production & Rehearsal Photography
© Steve Tanner

WISE CHILDREN

Emma Rice

WISE CHILDREN

Adapted for the stage
from the novel by Angela Carter

OBERON BOOKS
LONDON

WWW.OBERONBOOKS.COM

This adaptation first published in 2018 by Oberon Books Ltd
521 Caledonian Road, London N7 9RH
Tel: +44 (0) 20 7607 3637 / Fax: +44 (0) 20 7607 3629
e-mail: info@oberonbooks.com
www.oberonbooks.com

PB ISBN: 9781786826916
E ISBN: 9781786826923

Cover image: Hugo Glendinning
Cover design: Bob King Creative

Printed and bound by 4EDGE Limited, Hockley, Essex, UK.
eBook conversion by Lapiz Digital Services, India.

Visit www.oberonbooks.com to read more about all our books and to buy them. You
will also find features, author interviews and news of any author events, and you can
sign up for e-newsletters so that you're always first to hear about our new releases.

Printed on FSC accredited paper

10 9 8 7 6 5 4 3 2 1

For Simon Baker

Character Name	Brief Description	Age
Dora Chance	Ex-showgirl	75
Nora Chance	Ex-showgirl	75
Showgirl Dora	Glamorous showgirl	30s
Showgirl Nora	Glamorous showgirl	30s
Young Dora	Young girl	7/13
Young Nora	Young girl	7/13
Melchior Hazard	A grand stage actor	60/100
Young Melchior	A young actor	12/40
Peregrine Hazard	An adventurer and entrepreneur	60/100
Young Peregrine	A young adventurer	12/40
Grandma Chance	A theatrical landlady	
Lady Atalanta/Wheelchair	An aristocratic beauty married to Melchior Hazard	
Pretty Kitty	A chambermaid. Dora and Nora's mother	
Estella	A leading actress. Married to Ranulph Hazard. Melchior and Peregrine's mother	
Ranulph Hazard	An actor-manager. Married to Estella. Melchior and Peregrine's father	
Cassius Booth	A dashing romantic lead. Probably Melchior and Peregrine's real father	
Blue Eyed Boy	A blond tenor	
Saskia and Imogen Hazard	Melchior's twin daughters	
Prinking Minx	A RADA student	

All other parts played by the company

OPENING

Around the theatre, acrobats, clowns and dancers are putting on their make up and limbering up. They are old pros – a dab hand with a wig cap and some crimson lake. On the stage there is a caravan. Perhaps this raggle-taggle Corps de Ballet are on the road? Two girls arrive through the auditorium, they are twins and are about seven. They laugh, play and dance freely. The other performers start to encroach on the twin's space but the girls stop them in their tracks. They smile at the audience and we see a glimmer of animal power.

The GIRLS sing.

I have sharp teeth within my mouth,
Inside my dark red lips,
And polish bright hides my sharpened claws
In my finger tips.

And as I conceal my power,
All your strength is now on view.
You think you are possessing me–
But I've got my teeth in you.

PROLOGUE

The caravan door opens. We are in a house in Brixton. 49 Bard Street to be precise. The Corps de Ballet return to their dressing tables and carry on getting ready.

Three women live here. NORA is in her dressing gown. She is seventy-five and doing her ballet practice. A tiny person scoots around in a wheelchair. DORA is surrounded by papers, pictures, memorabilia and the ephemera of over a century in show business.

DORA

Why is London like Budapest?

The CHORUS shrug.

Because it is two cities divided by a river.

7

The CHORUS clap silently.

Good Evening! Let me introduce myself.
My name is Dora Chance. Welcome to
the wrong side of the tracks.

CHORUS

Sing:

We live on the wrong side of the tracks
Side of the tracks
Tread the worn out boards; avoid the cracks
Avoid the cracks

DORA

Me and Nora

NORA

That's me, Nora Chance.

DORA

We've always lived on the left hand side

NORA

The bastard side of Old Father Thames.

DORA

Once upon a time, you could make a
crude distinction, thus: the rich lived
amidst pleasant verdure in the North,
speedily whisked to exclusive shopping
by abundant public transport while the
poor eked out miserable existences in
the south, condemned to wait for hours
at windswept bus stops smelling of fish
and chips. But, you can't trust things to
stay the same. It's 1989 and there's been
a diaspora of the affluent; they jumped
into their diesel Saabs and dispersed
throughout the city. You'd never believe

8

the price of a house round here these days. And what does the robin do then poor thing?

NORA

Bugger the robin! What would have become of us, if Grandma hadn't left us this house? 49, Bard Road, Brixton, South West Two.

DORA

Bless this house. If it wasn't for this house, Nora and I would be on the streets by now, hauling our worldlies up and down in plastic bags, sucking on the bottle like babes unweaned, to gasp and freeze and finally snuff it disregarded on the street and blow away like rags.

NORA

That's a thought for a girl's seventy-fifth birthday, what? Yes! Seventy-five. Happy birthday to me. Born in this house just seventy-five years ago, today.

DORA

I made my bow five minutes ahead of Nora, My dearest sister. My dearest twin. Happy birthday to us.
We used to be song and dance girls.

NORA

And we can still lift a leg higher than your average dog if called for.

Both girls dance a short number.

9

DORA

> I feel in my ancient water, that something
> will happen today. Something exciting.
> Something nice, something nasty, I don't
> give a monkey's.

NORA

> Just as long as something happens to remind
> us we're still in the land of the living.

There is a gust of wind and a Stage Hand delivers an envelope to NORA and DORA.

DORA

> *(Reading.)* The Misses Dora and Nora
> Chance are invited to a celebration to mark
> the one hundredth birthday of Sir Melchior
> Hazard.

NORA

> Well I bleedin' never.

DORA

> A party! A big fat fancy party on the other
> side of the river. The smart side,
> the far side.

NORA

> Why now? What does the old bastard want
> with us now?

DORA

> Don't ask me.

NORA

> After seventy-five years? Something's not
> right.

DORA

> After seventy-five years? About bloomin' time.

NORA

I don't want to

DORA

Want to what?

NORA

Give him the satisfaction.

DORA

What about our satisfaction?

NORA

Oh Dora.

DORA

We're going.

NORA

When is it?

DORA

It's only tonight?

NORA

They've not given us much time to reply.

DORA

Does something make you think they
don't want us to go?

Both women laugh raucously.

The tiny person in a wheelchair whizzes around and boils over with splutters.

NORA

Hold hard ducky, we're never going to
leave you behind!

DORA

(To WHEELCHAIR.) Yes, Cinders, you shall
go to the ball.

NORA

Even if you aren't mentioned by name on the invite.

DORA

Let's have all the skeletons out of the closet, today, of all days! God knows we deserve a spot of bubbly after all these years.

DORA and NORA start to leave to get ready.

The CHORUS, mute but physical, manage to get DORA's attention.

What?

CHORUS

(In theatrical sign language.) What's happening?

NORA

You want to know what's happening?

The CHORUS nod theatrically.

DORA

Weren't you paying attention? We're going to a party! That's what's bloody happening! Melchior bloomin' Hazard's blinkin' 100th Birthday!

CHORUS

(In ballet sign language.) Who's he?

DORA

What? You don't know who Melchior Hazard is?

The CHORUS shake their heads.

NORA

You haven't heard of Melchior Hazard with whom, by a bizarre coincidence we share a birthday?

Another mute shake.

DORA

>Why, he's the finest actor of his generation!

The CHORUS are excited!

NORA

>The pillar of the legit!

They are faint with anticipation!

BOTH

>**Sir** Melchior Hazard no less.

A gust of wind brings the story and dancers into magical life!.

They sing 'There May be Trouble Ahead'.

ACT ONE

SCENE 1

DORA

> Now listen carefully. Like most family histories, this is a complicated affair and if you doze off now it's going to be a long evening! Sir Melchior Hazard is our natural father.

NORA

> Though you'd never guess it.

DORA

> But before we can even start to get a handle on him –

NORA

> The pretentious old git.

DORA

> We need to go back a generation. Ready? Good. Melchior's mother, our paternal grandmother, was born in a trunk in 1870.

ESTELLA pops her head out of the bed.

> She trod the boards from toddlerhood to an old stager of eight as a fairy. Lewis Carroll saw her, invited her for tea and got her to slip her frock off after the crumpets,

LEWIS CARROLL

> Slip off your frock dear and step this way. I'll take the teacup.

LEWIS CARROLL proceeds to snap her in the altogether.

NORA

> Here's the evidence, see? Not many people can boast a picture of their Grandmother posing for kiddiporn.

DORA

> She was called Estella and she sparkled as Juliet, Portia and Beatrice.

NORA

> Her hair was always coming undone, spraying out hairpins in all directions, her stockings half-mast, her petticoat adrift, her drawers drooping. She was a marvel and she was a mess.

ESTELLA

> I could do it all! Make you laugh, make you cry, sing, dance. Oh! But I was a fool for love!

DORA

> In 1888 came her big chance, to play Cordelia to the Lear of Ranulph Hazard.

RANULPH appears.

RANULPH

> One of the great roaring, actor-managers such as they don't make anymore!

ESTELLA

> A fool for love, I say!

DORA

> What an ecstasy the two of them provoked!

ESTELLA and RANULPH play out a scene from King Lear.

ESTELLA

O, look upon me, sir,
And hold your hands in benediction
o'er me:
No, sir, you must not kneel.

RANULPH

Pray, do not mock me:
I am a very foolish fond old man,
Fourscore and upward, not an hour
more nor less; And, to deal plainly,
I fear I am not in my perfect mind.
Do not laugh at me;
For, as I am a man, I think this lady
To be my child Cordelia.

ESTELLA

And so I am, I am.

CORDELIA and LEAR kiss passionately and inappropriately.

DORA

Old Ranulph was a good thirty years
older than Estella. All the same, they tied
the knot.

ESTELLA

But he was a drunk, a bankrupt and a
gambler. He'd fretted and philandered
and beaten and betrayed three wives
into early graves ahead of me.

RANULPH throws down a woman's corset.

RANULPH

Good riddance!

ESTELLA screams in frustration.

RANULPH

But no sacrificial lamb or shrinking violet she.

They fight.

She was a wild thing.

DORA

First of all he loved her madly and vice versa until Barnum (yes that Barnum!), made her an offer.

BARNUM

Hamlet.

CHORUS

Ooo, Hamlet.

RANULPH

She eyed me sideways wondering how I would take it,

ESTELLA

But he did me proud in a supporting role as Hamlet's father

CASSIUS BOOTH enters.

CASSIUS

Whilst a young, suave, athletic Cassius Booth stepped into the limelight beside her as Hamlet's best friend. Horatio.

ESTELLA and CASSIUS cavort flirtatiously as HORATIO and HAMLET.

HORATIO

Hillo, ho, ho, my lord!

HAMLET

Hillo, ho, ho, boy! come, bird, come.

HORATIO

What news, my lord?

HAMLET

O, wonderful!

HORATIO

Good my lord, tell it.

HAMLET

No; you'll reveal it.

HORATIO

Not I, my lord, by heaven.

HAMLET

But you'll be secret?

HORATIO

Ay, by heaven, my lord.

They make passionate love.

NORA

A female Hamlet is one thing, but a pregnant prince is quite another.

ESTELLA

Bugger

DORA

Now, Ranulph Hazard, during all of his lengthy marital and extra marital career had produced no issue, as yet, until his wife's transvestite Hamlet met her young Horatio.

CASSIUS

I'm off.

CASSIUS exits.

DORA

Yes! Tongues wagged but Ranulph's
twin boys were born. He named them
Melchior and Peregrine. Melchior and
Peregrine Hazard.

NORA

He loved his boys and cast them as the
princes in the tower as soon as they
could toddle.

RANULPH

**"Welcome, sweet princes, to London,
to your chamber."**

DORA

However, the old man was seized with
the desire to take Shakespeare where
Shakespeare had never been before.

RANULPH

I must take Shakespeare to the world.
Cairo, Caracas, Camarthen and beyond.

DORA

Estella, wings clipped by motherhood,
tagged on behind with her twin boys in
tow. The red haired woman with her
talent for making people happy, waved
goodbye to disappearing shore after
disappearing shore.

We see ESTELLA and her boys at the brow of an ocean liner.

Ranulph shouted at the world but it
would no longer listen to him.

RANULPH

Blow winds, blow! Crack thy Cheeks!

DORA

> Props and costumes were lost or stolen or fell to pieces and Ranulph drank, gambled and declaimed.

RANULPH

> **A horse a horse, my kingdom for a horse!**

DORA

> One night he gambled away his crown from Lear.
> Estella put together a new one for him out of a bit of cardboard.

ESTELLA gives the babies to NORA to look after whilst she makes RANULPH a new crown.

ESTELLA

> No one will know the difference.

DORA

> She dabbed on some gold paint.

ESTELLA kisses RANULPH tenderly and puts the crown on his head.

ESTELLA

> Here you are, my love. There, all better now.

CASSIUS back flips into this tender scene.

CASSIUS

> Hello Ranulph. Hello Estella.

NORA

> Will you look at those legs

CASSIUS

> Whilst you two have roamed yourselves to rags for the greater glory

of Shakespeare, I have rooted in one place and prospered. I am now an actor manager myself and have my very own theatre. London's sparkling Old Vic! **Give me your hands if we be friends and Robin will restore amends!**

The three take hands. The three Musketeers. The three Amigos.

NORA

What could possibly go wrong?

DORA

The play he picked was

NORA

Alas

DORA

Othello. All went well until bedtime after the first night party.

> **The poor soul sat sighing by a sycamore**
> **tree**
> **Sing willow, willow, willow**
> **Her hand on her bosom, her head on her**
> **knee**
>
> **The fresh streams ran by her, and**
> **murmer'd her moans**
> **Sing willow, willow, willow**
> **Her salt tears fell from her and softened**
> **the stones.**
>
> **Sing all a green willow, Willow, willow,**
> **willow**
> **Sing all a green willow**
> **My garland shall be.**

Let nobody blame him, his scorn I approve
Sing willow, willow, willow
He was born to be fair, I to die for his love
Sing willow, willow, willow
Sing willow, willow, willow
My garland shall be;

Sing all a green willow,
Willow, willow, willow
Sing all a green willow
My garland shall be.

I call'd my love false love
but what said he then?
If I court more women,
you'll couch with more men.

ESTELLA and CASSIUS start to make love RANULPH watches as they roll together.

RANULPH smothers ESTELLA, stabs CASSIUS, then shoots himself.

DORA

Exeunt Omnes.

The actors bow and exit.

NORA

But life goes on sister.

DORA

That it does.

SCENE 2

NORA throws the two red haired babies into the air and two red haired young boys land in their place.

NORA

> The two little orphans were stranded.

DORA

> Poor tragic waifs

NORA

> Even as scraps, these fellas were chalk and cheese.

DORA

> Melchior, our father, was all for art

MELCHIOR pens a poem.

NORA

> And Peregrine was out for fun.

PEREGRINE steals the paper and makes it into a butterfly.

DORA

> And don't think because they were brothers they liked each other.

They fight with a rage known only to near siblings.

NORA

> Alright you two break it up!

DORA

> So it was, as Wandsworth Workhouse threatened its icy grip, Peregrine gave a shrug and a wriggle and lickety-split was gone. Whoosh!

PEREGRINE vanishes.

NORA

Now Melchior had adored his father, worshipped him and took away from the catastrophe of his parents lives only one souvenir.

MELCHIOR crowns himself his father's successor with the pasteboard crown.

DORA

It was in his blood, wasn't it?

MELCHIOR

(To himself.)
To whom should I complain. Did I tell this. Who would believe me?
Those friends thou hast, and their adoption tried,
Grapple them to thy soul with hoops of steel; Give every man thy ear, but few thy voice;
Take each man's censure, but reserve thy judgment. Neither a borrower nor a lender be;
For loan oft loses both itself and friend, And borrowing dulls the edge of husbandry. This above all: to thine own self be true.

DORA

He found his way to a theatrical boarding house in Brixton.

NORA

49 Bard Road.

DORA

Where he first had the dubious pleasure of meeting.

24

DORA and NORA

> Grandma Chance.

MELCHIOR knocks on the door. GRANDMA CHANCE appears. She wears large bloomers, an industrial bra, lazy stockings and holds a bottle of crème de menthe.

GRANDMA

> Get the door, Pretty Kitty. Toot Sweet.
> I'm not getting any younger.

PRETTY KITTY opens the door to MELCHIOR. She gasps and falls deeply in love.

KITTY

> Good Day, Sir.

MELCHIOR

> Good Day, sweet lady.

GRANDMA

> Welcome to The Chance Boarding
> House for Theatricals down on their
> uppers. Or even down on the uppers of
> their uppers.

KITTY

> Can we help?

MELCHIOR

> I am hoping there might be room at the
> Inn?

KITTY

> Oh!

GRANDMA

> You've got stars in your eyes Kitty! Show
> Master... Master?

MELCHIOR

> Hazard. Melchior Hazard at your service, ladies.

GRANDMA

> Show Master Hazard to the attic room. Pay what you can, when you can, Ducky. We all rub along together here like family.

KITTY and MELCHIOR make their way up the winding stairs to his room.

DORA

> Brixton, before the lights went out over Europe, was the hub of a wheel of theatres, music halls, Empires, Royalties, what have you. You could tram it all over from Brixton. The streets of tall narrow houses were stuffed to the brim with stand-up comics; adagio dancers; soubrettes; conjurers; fiddlers; speciality acts with dogs, doves; dwarfs; goats, you name it.

As she speaks, performers and animals pop out from baskets and clothes piles. They watch as KITTY and MELCHIOR find themselves in the attic bedroom.

> I suppose Kitty must have fallen fast and deep for this poor, handsome, starving boy. I wonder how she did it?
> Shyly?

We see her make love shyly.

> Lewdly?

We see her make love lewdly.

> I'd like to think it went like this.

KITTY unwraps MELCHIOR's crown, puts it on her head and they make joyous, athletic, surprising love.

You always like to think that a bit of love, or a least a little pleasure went into your making, but I will never know.

NORA

His theatre doorstep vigils and auditions must have paid off, for Melchior Hazard and his cardboard crown were gone by the time our mother missed her first period.

MELCHIOR exits.

KITTY

Bugger.

NORA

Nine months later we came bursting out.

Two babies are throw into KITTY's arms by a departing MELCHIOR.

DORA

It was a Monday morning and a day of sunshine and high winds. Seventy-five years ago today when the zeppelins were falling.

NORA

Grandma always said that our mother took a good look at us, two wee bawling baby girls, and smiled.

DORA

Why would she have smiled? She was just seventeen, no man, no home and there was a war on.

GRANDMA

> Why shouldn't she smile? She hadn't got
> a mum or a dad, but a baby was the next
> best thing.

KITTY gasps.

DORA

> Her heart gave out just after we made
> our entrance, mine just five minutes
> ahead of Nora.

KITTY gasps.

> The doctor arrived soon after, but it was
> too late.

KITTY dies.

> Kitty, like a little stray cat.

*GRANDMA CHANCE takes the babies from dead KITTY, covers her gently
and takes the girls to the window. NORA and DORA follow their baby
selves to the window.*

GRANDMA

> My beautiful babes, my precious bundles.

Washing appears.

> Look, look… Monday, washday. What a
> sight! Long black stockings stepping out
> with gent's long johns. French knickers
> doing the CanCan with the frilly
> petticoats… Look, look…

DORA

> And so, the first thing we saw with our
> swimming baby eyes was sunshine and
> dancing. She turned us away from the sight
> of our poor lifeless mother and showed us
> the world and its simple pleasures.

NORA

Lucky for us, Grandma took to children like a duck to water. I asked her once why she'd never had babies of her own. She said:

GRANDMA

I'd often wondered what men were for. Then I had one cuddle of you two and the penny finally dropped.

DORA

She never let us call her Mother out of respect for the dead.

NORA

We called her 'Grandma'

DORA

And 'Chance' became our handle.

NORA

(To the audience.) Yes. Misses Nora and Dora Chance, yours truly, are Sir Melchior Hazard's daughters.

DORA

His natural daughters.

NORA

His never-by-him officially recognized daughters. We girls are illegitimate in every way.

DORA

As I said, welcome to the wrong side of the tracks.

NORA and DORA look again at the invitation to MELCHIOR's party. The washing, babies and KITTY disappear leaving us back in the present.

SCENE 3

WHEELCHAIR whizzes about in a state of anxiety about the party.

DORA

> Steady on, Wheelchair. There's hours before we have to leave.

NORA

> Pace yourself as Grandma used to say.

DORA

> Our beloved Grandma Chance was a convert to naturism

GRANDMA appears, buck-naked.

NORA

> She thought it was good for us kiddies to get air and sunlight on our skins as well.

Buck-naked DORA and NORA appear. They are about five years old.

DORA

> We saved a lot on wear and tear on clothes though!

GRANDMA

> Now! What new words have you learnt today? Nora?

YOUNG NORA

> Vegetarianism

GRANDMA

> Dora?

YOUNG DORA

> Pacifism.

GRANDMA

Good girls. I'll make revolutionaries of you yet!

There is a loud knocking at the door.

Get the door, Noradora. Toot sweet!
I'm not getting any younger!

The girls back flip and cartwheel to the door and open it to reveal PEREGRINE HAZARD. He is handsome, huge, red headed and carrying a wooden box.

PEREGRINE

Hello Girls! *(To GRANDMA.)* Hello.

DORA

Oooh, Peregrine was a handsome man.
Glorious, broad of shoulder, heavy of thigh
and that unruly thatch of burnished copper
hair. Oooh.

GRANDMA

What the fuck!

GRANDMA realizes that she is naked. Embarrassed, she excuses herself and then reappears, this time with a bra on. Still embarrassed she leaves again and returns with knickers on as well.

Do I know you, sir? You look, somehow
familiar.

PEREGRINE

My dear lady, I am Peregrine Hazard, the
twin brother of Melchior Hazard.

GRANDMA

I knew it! That explains it. That sneaky,
dirty, lying, pretentious, hypocritical, randy,
pompous little scrap of an excuse for a
man? Get out. Out I tell you! We have no

31

PEREGRINE

need for the likes of you and him in this
'ouse. OUT!

My dear woman, hear me out! I really
couldn't agree more with your analysis
of his character, except you are far
kinder than I would be if I were asked to
describe my dearest brother in words.

GRANDMA

You give me hope for the human race,
Peregrine.

PEREGRINE

I come bearing news of his impending
marriage to Lady Atalanta Lynde,

DORA

Remember that name ladies and gents

PEREGRINE

She is an old friend of mine, and what
is more, he wants me to come to some
arrangement with you and your delightful
girls to avoid any future embarrassment.

GRANDMA

An arrangement? He's changed his tune!
I bearded the bastard in his den after a
matinee of Romeo only the other day. He
was at a disadvantage as he only had his
tights and some mascara on, but he still
denied paternity. The two faced little shit.

PEREGRINE

Between you and me, I believe he's
afraid that you'll show up at the wedding
with the girls in tow.

GRANDMA

Tell me more about this "arrangement".

Newly bonded, the family snuggle up. GRANDMA pours PEREGRINE a drink and the two naked girls sit on his lap. They make a fine picture of freedom and naughtiness.

PEREGRINE

Ladies, you should all know that your father's bride –

DORA

Lady Atalanta Lynde

PEREGRINE

– is loaded.

He produces a coin from behind NORA's ear and gives it to her.

He, therefore, is also now loaded.

He produces another from behind DORA's and pops it in her hand. NORA goes and plays with her coin!

GRANDMA

Well, he's welcome to unload some of his ill-gotten gains on us! If you haven't got a ticket, you can't win, me old duck. Remember the Russian proverb: "Hope for the best, expect the worst" All together now!

ALL

Hope for the best, expect the worst!

PEREGRINE and five-year-old DORA look at each other. It is love at first sight.

DORA

And so it was that I first met my Uncle Peregrine as naked as the day I was born.

33

PEREGRINE

> Let's have some music.

PEREGRINE goes to the wooden box that he brought with him and opens it to reveal a beautiful toy theatre for the girls to play with. He puts a disc on the gramophone. 'I Can't Give you Anything but Love' starts to play. He sings along and the girls start to dance.

PEREGRINE

> Come on Nora and Dora, I'm going to teach you how to dance. I think you're naturals! You're going to be shining stars!

He dances with the girls as they climb all over him like hairless squirrels. He puts his hand out to GRANDMA and they dance together like bread that has found its butter.

DORA

> And there we were, all dancing, to a song that made us a promise our father never kept.

NORA

> And, as for us, we haven't stopped dancing since, have we, Dora?

They sing 'I Can't Give You Anything But Love' by Red Garland.

DORA and NORA

> What a joy it is to dance and sing!
> ...*love*

DORA

> After all that, it was Peregrine, not Melchior, who did the gentlemanly thing. His name was on the cheques that began to arrive on the first of every month. When quizzed, he said that Melchior had decided to give out that

34

it was Peregrine that had done the dirty deed and that she, Grandma Chance, had gone down as our mother to keep the accountants happy.

GRANDMA

They've as good as married us off!

PEREGRINE and GRANDMA hoot with laughter.

NORA

And so, from that day on, Peregrine came and went from our lives. He was a dutiful 'father', paying for dancing lessons, tap shoes and bringing us parcels from Harrods and Hamleys.

DORA

Of course, he never stayed. A man like that has a very low boredom threshold, the wonderlust would seize him by the throat and he would leave for years at a time.

PEREGRINE leaves.

NORA

The cheques kept coming though. Regular as clockwork.

The heavy, red, velvet curtain falls in front of DORA, leaving only a glow at the bottom of the curtain.

DORA

(*From behind the curtain.*)
Oi! Who dropped that in? Bloody stage hands, I'll have you and your overtime!

SCENE 4

DORA and NORA tap dance to the front of the curtain.

DORA

> Now where were we?

NORA

> We're at the theatre

DORA

> How old are we?

NORA

> We are seven!

GRANDMA brings on a big, eccentric home-made cake with seven candles. She presents it to YOUNG DORA and YOUNG NORA who are dressed up in their best clothes and have their eyes closed.

CHORUS

> *(Sing.)* Happy birthday dear Noradora.
> Happy Birthday to you

GRANDMA

> Make a wish Noradora.

They blow out the candles and then open their eyes. Their wish has been granted!

YOUNG NORA

> We're at the theatre.

YOUNG DORA

> I can't believe it. Lady Be Good at
> The Old Vic!

YOUNG NORA

> I think I might faint.

YOUNG DORA

> Look at the curtain. It's teasing us, Nor!

YOUNG NORA

Look how the bottom of it glows. I want to touch it.

YOUNG DORA

What's behind it?

YOUNG NORA

Whatever it is will be wonderful

YOUNG DORA

Whatever it is I can taste in the air, smell it in the creases of the velvet.

YOUNG DORA and YOUNG NORA feel their hearts.

YOUNG DORA
and YOUNG NORA

Pit a pat. Pit a pat

GRANDMA

You've got stars in your eyes girls!

Two STAGEHANDS enter.

STAGEHAND

You can't be up on the stage.

STAGEHAND 2

It's against the rules.

STAGEHAND

Right. You deal with the old baggage, I'll take the kids

GRANDMA

Get your hands off me!

In the scuffle, GRANDMA spots MELCHIOR.

NORA

Then, like a dog spotting a rabbit,
Grandma froze.

*GRANDMA shaking with rage, slowly raises her finger to point at someone
or something in the Dress Circle.*

DORA

If you'd drawn a straight line from the
end of her finger into the dress circle, it
would have landed on a very handsome,
tall, dark young man.

*The man in question (MELCHIOR HAZARD) is accompanied by a very
elegant young woman (LADY ATALANTA LYNDE). All clean lines and
sophistication.*

YOUNG DORA

Grandma, What is it?

YOUNG NORA

Grandma, Who is it?

GRANDMA

That man is… your father!

*The Girls look up at MELCHIOR and are transfixed. He sees them,
but looks away.*

Oi! You! Can't you even look your own
children in the eye? You heard what
I said, no need to look around. You!
I'm talking to you. Remember me?
Remember rubbing along together at my
place? You sneaky, lying, pretentious,
little shit…. Look at them. Look at them!

The USHER tries to restrain her.

USHER

Please Madame! Take your seats.

All eyes are on this elderly lady and her two small girls.

GRANDMA

        Come on Girls, we need to get out of
here.

*GRANDMA drags the young girls through the theatre and out of the
auditorium leaving DORA and NORA on stage. Still looking at their father
the band strikes up and DORA sings a slow version of 'Lady Be Good'*

GRANDMA and the girls arrive home.

GRANDMA

        (To herself.) Damn Damn Damn Damn.

YOUNG NORA

        Grandma?

GRANDMA

        (Sharply.) What? *(To herself.)* Damn Damn
Damn Damn Damn Damn.

YOUNG NORA

        You said that man …

GRANDMA

        What man?

YOUNG DORA

        The one you pointed at

GRANDMA

        Melchior Hazard?

YOUNG DORA
and YOUNG NORA

        Pit a pit, pit a pat

GRANDMA

        What about him?

YOUNG DORA

You said …

GRANDMA

I said what?

YOUNG NORA

You said that he was our father.

GRANDMA

Yes dammit. He bloody well is – and
don't you let anyone tell you differently.

YOUNG DORA

What is a 'father' Grandma?

GRANDMA

What?

YOUNG NORA

Tell us what a 'father' is.

YOUNG DORA

And what does someone have to do to
become a father?

GRANDMA

Bloody Hell. Listen up girls, There's no
dressing up what I am about to tell you.
Have you heard of the word 'Prong?'

YOUNG DORA
and YOUNG NORA

Prong?

*There follows a demonstration of different sorts of intercourse improvised
with items from GRANDMA's handbag.*

GRANDMA

A and A make pleasure
A and B make trouble

> *B and B make fireworks*
> *That pop like a a bubble*

If you would like to lead a blameless life –
avoid sexual intercourse like the plague.

CHORUS

> *A and A make pleasure*
> *A and B make trouble*
> *B and B make fireworks*
> *That pop like a bubble*

DORA sings 'Lady Be Good' by Ella Fitzgerald simultaneously.

DORA

    Like a bubble.

NORA and DORA wriggle and giggle.

GRANDMA

    Now…. What do unicorns and virgins
    have in common?

YOUNG DORA
and YOUNG NORA

    We don't know. What do unicorns and
    virgins have in common?

GRANDMA

    They are both fabulous beasts and don't
    you forget it!

She cuddles them and tickles their tummies.

SCENE 5

A STAGEHAND puts down a bucket of sand. We are at Brighton Beach.

DORA

Bloody Hell! Are we at Brighton already? The years are slipping through our fingers like sand, Nor. We can't be at Brighton yet! It was an August bank holiday 1927, we would have just turned thirteen. Peregrine roared up in a cab.

PEREGRINE

Keep the meter running!

YOUNG DORA
and YOUNG NORA

(Running up to him with excitement.) Uncle Perry!

PEREGRINE

You look peaky girls! Can't have that.

DORA

Peregrine made up for everything! He always came back. Always.

PEREGRINE

Dr Brighton is the cure for all! Oh! I've missed my girls!

He hands GRANDMA a bottle of Champagne.

GRANDMA

Champagne to all here, real pain to the other bastards!

ALL

Real pain to the other bastards.

PEREGRINE

> To the beach! All aboard!

YOUNG NORA, YOUNG DORA and GRANDMA all pile into the cab and set off. They arrive at Brighton beach.

GRANDMA

> Oh! Smell that! All clean, cool and salty!
> Right, let's get these shoes and socks
> off – I love to feel the tickle and glitter of
> salt water on my feet!

YOUNG NORA starts to play and dance on the sand.

YOUNG DORA

> Uncle Perry, what's that big white pigeon?

PEREGRINE

> That's a seagull!

YOUNG DORA

> What's that?

PEREGRINE

> That's an ice cream van

YOUNG DORA

> And what's that wooden thing in the sea
> that looks like a castle?

PEREGRINE

> That's the Pier.

YOUNG DORA

> What happens on the Pier, Uncle Perry?

The people on the beach go into slow motion as GORGEOUS GEORGE appears and tells a joke.

GORGEOUS GEORGE

> Thank you very much ladies and
> gentlemen. I expected more but I'm
> satisfied. Welcome to Brighton Pier,
> my name is George, Gorgeous George
> – there will never be another! They all
> laughed when I said I wanted to be a
> comedian – they're not laughing now!
>
> I just got back from my holidays – I went
> to Blackpool. I went looking for a room
> and I went and knocked on a door.
> A lady answered, a nice lady; a little bit
> more, not so much and then perhaps.
> It's all I need, a bit of encouragement.
> I said can you accommodate me? She
> said: No I'm fully booked! I said surely
> you can squeeze me in your little back
> room. She said "I could but I haven't got
> time for that now".

Back at the beach.

YOUNG DORA

> I want to go to the pier! I want to dance
> on Brighton pier!

PEREGRINE

> Well we'd better find out if you are good
> enough! Show us what you can do, my
> little chorines! Let's see if those dancing
> lessons have paid off!

*All the people on the beach start to form a band and play the Black
Bottom. DORA and NORA dance joyfully on the sand, UNCLE PERRY
juggles whilst GRANDMA laughs and drinks champagne. The dancing
freezes and GORGEOUS GEORGE picks up his act again.*

GORGEOUS GEORGE

Ere! I was walking down a very narrow
mountain path. So narrow no one can
pass by. When in the distance I saw a
beautiful brunette walking towards me.
Not a stitch on – that's right Mrs not a
stitch! Cor Blimey, I didn't know whether
to toss myself off or block her passage.

*Back at the beach, the girls start to dance again and the beach erupts
with applause. When the girls take their bows, UNCLE PERRY takes
round his boater.*

PEREGRINE

Buy us a cup of tea girls! You can
afford it! What a couple of pros you've
become!

YOUNG DORA

I don't want a cup of tea. I want to see
Gorgeous George!

They go to the end of pier to see GORGEOUS GEORGE finish his routine.

GORGEOUS GEORGE

Where are all you latecomers from?

YOUNG DORA
and YOUNG NORA

Brixton!

GORGEOUS GEORGE

Where in Brixton?

YOUNG DORA
and YOUNG NORA

49 Bard Road!

GORGEOUS GEORGE

I had theatrical digs in Bard Road once –
a very accommodating landlady I seem
to remember... but back to the show.
When I was young I said to my dad
"I want to get married". He said,
"Who to"? I said, "Miss Green". He said
"You can't". I said "Why?" He said "You
can't she's your half sister. When I was
young I had a bike, I got about a bit".
I said "Okay, I'll marry Miss White".
He said "You can't she's your half sister
too". So I walked about a bit, dejected
like, when my mother said "What's the
matter son?" I said "I wanted to marry
Miss Green but Dad says that she's my
half sister. So I said that I wanted to
marry Miss White but Dad said that
she's my half sister too and I don't know
what to do."
My mother said "Marry who you want
son! He's not your father!"

The show ends and GORGEOUS GEORGE exits.

DORA

I've been happy before and I've been
happy after, but that day, on Brighton pier
was the first time I was old enough and
wise enough to know my own feelings.

YOUNG DORA

Goodness, I'm happy.

PEREGRINE

Fancy a stroll ladies?

GRANDMA

> I'm popping backstage. I'm going to get
> George to butter my baps.

PEREGRINE and the GIRLS set off.

PEREGRINE

> *(Seeing something that stops him in his tracks.)*
> Shit.

DORA

> If you'd drawn a straight line from his
> dark eyes, it would have landed on a
> theatre poster.

YOUNG DORA

> *(Reading.)* 'Melchior Hazard and
> company in *Macbeth.*'

*YOUNG DORA and YOUNG NORA hide their faces, as if shy of the poster.
PEREGRINE makes them look him in the eyes.*

PEREGRINE

> You do know that you ain't my girls.
> I am not now, nor ever have been your
> father. No. And you do know, don't you,
> that he –
>
> *(He gestures to the picture.)*
>
> …Is.

DORA

> We knew that Melchior Hazard was our
> father, but now we also knew…

NORA

> Since Grandma Chance had talked us
> through the facts of life.

DORA

What it was father did, where he'd
done it, and who he'd done it to. We
knew it all. And here he was playing
Shakespeare, whilst we were fresh from
singing on the street.

NORA

We'd never felt so illegitimate in our lives.

PEREGRINE sees the pain in the girls' faces.

YOUNG DORA

Let's get back to Grandma

DORA

But more than anything else in the
world, I longed to feast my eyes on the
sight of my father.

*YOUNG DORA reaches out for YOUNG NORA's hand. They hang on to
each other tight.*

PEREGRINE

Dammit! Come with me.

*PEREGRINE whisks the girls into MELCHIOR's dressing room. It is an
Aladdin's cave. His razor, his greasepaint, his mirror, his towel. There
is a photo of LADY ATALANTA LYNDE. So elegant.*

*The play is over and MELCHIOR bursts into his dressing room as if he
had flown from the stage on wires.*

*The world stands still as MELCHIOR's eyes skid over the smiling, eager
and desperate girls.*

MELCHIOR

Peregrine! How nice of you to come and
visit me!

DORA

> In all my life no disappointment ever after
> measured up to it. He did not see us, even
> as we sat there glowing with expectation.

MELCHIOR and PEREGRINE stare each other out.

MELCHIOR

> How have you been, brother? It's been
> too long.

PEREGRINE

> Don't you bloody well dare, Melchior.

He gestured to the GIRLS.

MELCHIOR

> And you've brought your lovely daughters
> too!

DORA and NORA

> Pit a pat. Pit a pat

MELCHIOR

> Did I tell you, dear brother? Atalanta is
> expecting! I shall also be a father soon
> and I shall dote on any child of mine
> more than life itself.

PEREGRINE roars like a tiger.

DORA

> I have a memory, although I know it
> cannot be a true one, that Peregrine swept
> us up into his arms. That when our father
> denied us, Peregrine spread his arms as
> wide as wings and gathered us up. And
> then, hup, he did a back flip out of the
> window and flew away with us, crushed
> against his soft, warm belly, saving us.

Perhaps I am imagining the back flip.

PEREGRINE

My dear, beautiful, tender girls.

NORA

Truly, what he did was this…

PEREGRINE holds his arms out to the girls and they scamper to harbour, whimpering.

PEREGRINE

It is a Wise Child that knows its own father, but wiser yet, the father who knows his own child.

DORA

We cried so much we couldn't see our way back to the voluminous arms of Grandma.

The GIRLS dive into GRANDMA CHANCE's arms.

PEREGRINE gently pulls YOUNG DORA out of the embrace and kneels at her feet. GRANDMA and YOUNG NORA don't seem to notice she has gone. He places his hands on her ankles and starts to run them slowly upwards.

YOUNG DORA

> *And as I conceal my power,*
> *All your strength is now on view.*
> *You think you are possessing me –*
> *But I've got my teeth in you*
> *In you*

PEREGRINE pulls down YOUNG DORA's pants.

SCENE 6

NORA

> Lady Atalanta gave birth to the twins on
> the same day that our periods started

YOUNG DORA and YOUNG NORA drop their red pants. Two red headed babies are delivered to LADY ATALANTA whilst YOUNG NORA and YOUNG DORA watch, red pants half mast.

LADY ATALANTA is delighted. The Girls, less so.

DORA

> I always think it was a mean, dirty
> trick that connected their birth and our
> puberty. We turned into women, the
> very day that they turned into babies.
> We've never been equals.
> They've always had the edge on us.

NORA

> So rich

DORA

> So well-connected

NORA

> So legitimate

DORA

> Sod all that

BOTH

> So young.

We see LADY ATALANTA and MELCHIOR create the perfect family scene.

MELCHIOR

> My beautiful Atalanta, you are so clever.
> So very, very clever. My darling Saskia,

my darling Imogen. My very own
'Darling Buds of May'!

He cherishes his wife and caresses his beloved babes.

GRANDMA

Darling buds of May? Bloody 'ell.

MELCHIOR

**"My bounty is as boundless as the sea,
My love as deep. The more I give to
thee, the more I have, for both are
infinite"**

DORA

It was around this time that Uncle Perry
lost all his moolah on the Wall Street crash.

We see UNCLE PEREGRINE get the shirt stripped from his back.

PEREGRINE

You'll have to earn your own keep now,
my little Chorines. Forgive me.

He is whisked away by men he clearly owes money to.

DORA

So needs must, we got a job. Panto in
Kennington.

NORA

Chorus girls in red shoes.

GRANDMA

Two pounds a week each. It went a long
way in those days.

*The stage fills with the Pantomime company in rehearsal. They are
working on the dance break for 'Yes, My Darling Daughter'.*

DIRECTOR

> Jump, jump, jump. Show those teeth,
> kick those legs, lift that bale!

CLOWN

> Time for the slosh scene?

DIRECTOR

> Not yet! Starting positions, they've
> opened the house.

The curtain drops but from behind it we hear a sudden flutter and fuss amongst the company. There is much peeking through the curtains.

A PIERROT

> It's only Lady Atalanta Hazard and the
> darling buds of May! Theatrical royalty
> I tell you.

A HOOFER

> See her dress.

A CLOWN

> It must be French, from Paris.

A PIERROT

> She has come to see us!

A HOOFER

> To see our humble show!

A CLOWN

> Oh Lord!

YOUNG NORA

> I wont go on! I won't! What humiliation,
> that fucking frock in a box, looking down
> her pompous snout at us. ...
> Never, never. I quit.

YOUNG NORA throws herself on the floor in a rage. The company, unimpressed, pick her up and push her on.

CLOWN

Anyone got a birthday?

DORA

The show went on of course and so did we.

They start to perform 'Yes My Darling Daughter'. Half way through the action stops and time stands still.

LADY ATALANTA

(From the box.) As soon as I set eyes on them, I knew. I could see Melchior in their eyes, Melchior in their cheeks and Melchior in their legs. I checked the programme and it only confirmed the truth. Peregrine had told me of them when we, when we... When we were friends. My heart almost burst when I looked across the footlights at the daughters that were not mine.

Handing the flowers across the audience.

Pleases please, give these to the girls, hand them to the wonderful dancing girls.

The flowers are passed through the audience and given to YOUNG DORA.

YOUNG DORA

(Accepting the flowers.) Who are they from? Who?

The audience explain that they are from LADY ATALANTA HAZARD.

Thank you Ma'am. Thank you.

YOUNG DORA curtseys.

YOUNG NORA

(Taking the flowers.) Forget-me-knots?
You can keep your rotten flowers. Forget
– me-knots? Give them to your husband,
he is the one who is forgetful. Fuck you.
Fuck you both.

She throws the flowers down and storms off the stage into the dressing room.

Smoke and mirrors, Dor. That's all we
are. Smoke and fucking mirrors.

She cries tears of deep rage.

YOUNG DORA

You're not smoke and mirrors to me Nor.
You're the best, you're my best.

YOUNG NORA

The best? Really? Every bone in our
bodies aching?

YOUNG DORA

Feet burning.

YOUNG NORA

Exhausted.

YOUNG DORA

Propping against each other on the night
tram after work, half asleep, half awake?

YOUNG NORA

Face it Dor, we're the bottom of the pile
and always will be. If we didn't keep
pushing, no one would look at us twice.

YOUNG DORA

On our own, maybe. But, put us
together, Nor. Put us together...

55

The young women hold on to each other for dear life.

DORA

> After that night, we decided that we
> needed a little something extra to make
> us stand out.

GRANDMA

> *(Drinking a glass of stout.)* Not, blonde. No.
> Not red. Black! The Chance Girls need
> some Spanish Ebony and a bit of a trim.

The girls wrap their long mousy hair in towels and GRANDMA administers the dye. There is much washing, crying and scissor snipping before they are revealed with sharp, black bobs.

> Nora, you shall wear Shamilar and Dora,
> you shall wear Mitsouko. Ladies and
> Gentlemen, I give you... The Lucky
> Chances!

Out from the towels emerge a new, sassy look. Black bobs!

GRANDMA gives them perfume and they spray themselves sexually. The childhood has fallen from them and they are stars.

The audience applauds as the girls sing 'Yes my Darling Daughter'.

YOUNG DORA and NORA are swapped half way through the song for SHOW DORA and SHOW NORA. They are magnificent and in their prime!

They are centre stage, they are in charge. They are brilliant!

They leap into the audience at the end and embrace the crowd. They accept flowers and cards and kisses.

SCENE 7

SHOW NORA pulls a man onto the stage and starts to dance freely with him. They tango with ferocity. She loves the passion and limelight.

DORA

> Look at her! Nora was always free with it and threw her heart away as if it were a used bus ticket. She had a passion to know about life and all its dirty corners. A sort of grand carelessness possessed her each time she fell in love. She opened up, she melted down at the first touch, the first kiss; each time she fell in love, she fell for the first time.

She casts aside the man and picks out the drummer who dances with her and drums rhythms on her body.

> When she dated the drummer she was black and blue.

SHOW NORA

> Love-taps

DORA

> Preserve me from the passion of a percussionist.
> And when she fell in love, contraception was the last thing on her mind.

SHOW DORA

> Dutch Cap?

SHOW DORA hands SHOW NORA a small bag with a dutch cap in.

SHOW NORA

> *(Throwing it away.)* Bob off, Dora!

CHORUS

> *(Singing.) She loves the game, she loves the chase*
> *She welcomes each advance,*
> *Each sleight of foot and change of place,*
> *Each figure in the dance.*
>
> *And when the game turns into war,*
> *He takes out his long knife –*
> *Concealing what he meant it for,*
> *Which is, to take her life*

The dance with the PERCUSSIONIST reaches a violent sexual frenzy. Blood begins to pool on the stage. The music stops and both SHOW NORA and the PERCUSSIONIST look down in horror. The drummer walks away. He wants nothing to do with this mess.

SHOW NORA puts her hands in the blood and wails. A spotlight picks out her grief.

SHOW NORA

No. Please no.

She tries to get out of the light but the spot follows her.

No.

She is utterly bereft.

SHOW DORA

Don't cry. These things happen, Nor. It'll be okay. It'll be for the best. You wouldn't have been able to go out in the evenings anymore. Or dance.

SHOW NORA

I wouldn't have cared.

SHOW DORA

I'd have cared. It would be no fun going out without you. Dancing without you. We've still got each other.

58

SHOW DORA picks up SHOW NORA and cleans her up. She wipes the floor and NORA's hands and legs. She sings quietly 'I Can't Give You Anything but Love, Baby'.

DORA

After the miscarriage she went around
with a face like a month of Sundays for
all of three weeks.

SHOW NORA spots someone in the audience.

NORA

Then whoops!

She pulls a beautiful young man out of the crowd and starts to dance with him. He is young and blond, with eyes as blue as the sky. THE BLUE EYED BOY.

DORA

Head over heels again!

She kisses him passionately as DORA looks on.

NORA

He was a scrap of a lad, pale as a lily,
blonde as a chick.

DORA

And eyes as blue as sky. He didn't know
what had hit him.

SHOW NORA takes the lad into the dressing room and makes loud love to him as SHOW DORA waits outside and listens, at first in disbelief, and then with interest.

GRANDMA CHANCE enters with a birthday cake. This time there are seventeen candles.

GRANDMA and DORA

Nora! Nora!!!

SHOW NORA reappears, flushed from her dressing room activity. The BLUE EYED BOY appears behind her. SHOW DORA cannot take her eyes off him. They smile at each other, then the boy scampers away.

GRANDMA

Make a wish!

The girls blow out the candles and a make a wish. GRANDMA leaves them to eat their cake.

SHOW DORA

Nora...

SHOW NORA

Yes?

SHOW DORA

Give me your fella as a birthday present.

SHOW NORA

Get you own fella

SHOW DORA

He's the only one I want Nora. I'll only do it once.

SHOW NORA

Bob off, Dor.

SHOW DORA

I'll give him back, promise. He's crazy about you and has never given me a second look.

SHOW NORA

He'll know the difference then.

SHOW DORA

We won't know until we try. Same eyes, same mouth, same hair. Please, Nor.

SHOW NORA

If it was only the once…

SHOW DORA

I'll keep my mouth shut. He's as
innocent as asparagus. Why should he
guess? Nora, I want him so.

SHOW NORA

Oh Dora

SHOW DORA

Wait.

*The young women swap perfumes and SHOW NORA gets the BLUE
EYED BOY from the wings. She switches off the lights and swaps with
SHOW DORA.*

DORA

I smelled the unfamiliar perfume on my
skin and felt voluptuous. I wanted him
more than anything.

*SHOW DORA sings 'The Way You Look Tonight' by Frank Sinatra, and
kneels at his feet of the BLUE EYED BOY. She touches his ankles and
runs her hands up his thigh. He kneels down to join her and they make
love. Tender, fresh, simple and young.*

He never said 'Nora, there's something
different about you, something more
enchanting, tonight'. I'll never know if
he could tell the difference.

*The BLUE EYED BOY kisses SHOW DORA and leaves. SHOW NORA
comes in and snuggles up with her twin.*

SHOW DORA

Thank you, Nor.

SHOW NORA

You owe me.

SHOW DORA

Do you love him?

SHOW NORA

Don't start that Dora. You promised it
would just be the once.

SHOW DORA

Do you?

SHOW NORA

It doesn't matter. They never stay
anyway.

*The doors of the theatre burst open and harsh light falls on the women.
They shield their eyes. The huge figure of MELCHIOR is silhouetted with
LADY ATALANTA.*

MELCHIOR

Strange how potent cheap music is! But!
**"If music be the food of love, play on.
Give me excess of it"**

DORA and NORA

Pit a pat. Pit a pat.

Clearly egged on by LADY ATALANTA, MELCHIOR bows.

LADY ATALANTA

Happy Birthday, Lucky Chances.

SHOW DORA bursts into tears.

MELCHIOR

Don't cry, young lady. I have a birthday
present for you both. A job offer. I want
you both to appear alongside me in my
soon-to-be-famous Shakespearean revue...

'What you Will!' It's a brave new world
and we must keep up with the times.

SHOW DORA
& SHOW NORA

Yes! Yes!

MELCHIOR

I think you have exactly the common
touch that I need.

SHOW DORA
& SHOW NORA

Common touch

PEREGRINE

Hello Girls!

SHOW NORA
& SHOW DORA

Uncle Perry!

PEREGRINE

Did you miss me? You didn't think that
I would abandon my Lucky Chances on
their birthday did you? And we're going
to be working together! I'm investing in
'What You Will!'

LADY ATALANTA

I think this calls for a celebration!

*SHOW DORA and MELCHIOR dance, he blows SHOW NORA a kiss and
in a jiffy, he, PEREGRINE and LADY ATALANTA are gone.*

SHOW DORA

Did that just happen?

SHOW NORA

I'm not sure

DORA

I had made love to a boy for the first time my father had danced with me for the first time

NORA

And our names would be up in lights on Shaftesbury Avenue for the first time.

They whoop and dance with pleasure.

SHOW NORA

We're going to be stars!

SHOW DORA

He wants us!

DORA

Not as daughters.

SHOW NORA

He wants us!

DORA

But as long-legged, ever smiling, unquestioning Showgirls.

**SHOW DORA
& SHOW NORA**

Our Father, wants us!

NORA

What could possibly go wrong?

END OF ACT ONE.

ACT TWO

SCENE 1

We return to the theatre and it is time for curtain up on 'What You Will'. The bottom of the tabs glow provocatively.

GRANDMA

Ladies and Gentlemen, please put your hands together for our greatest living Shakespearean (although he has always steered clear of Hamlet, nervous that the critics might think he wasn't half the man his mother had been!)
My favourite play by Shakespeare is As You Lick It. And let's face it who doesn't like to lick it, or occasionally I like to flick it particularly when I am Taming my Shrew. But I do draw the line at anything entering my Coriolanus –

PEREGRINE enters to avoid further embarrassment.

PEREGRINE

I give you The one and only Melchior Hazard who is joined this evening by... the Lucky Chances!

The curtain rises.

MELCHIOR

"All the world's a stage,
And all the men and women merely players;
They all have their entrances and exits,
And each man in his time plays many parts."

WHAT YOU WILL – GIRLS WILL BE BOYS

SHOW NORA and SHOW DORA are revealed looking dapper and sexy in Shakespearean mens' clothing…

> *Whilst we've never had a problem*
> *Understanding Willy*
> *His cross-dressing habit was simply*
> *overkill – He*
> *Dipped his quill in all he fancied*
> *Hose, or ruff, or frill –*
> *Was he being trans–a–curious*
> *Or simply*
> *What You Will?*
>
> *Chorus*
> *Girls will be Boys when they want*
> *their own way*
> *Men take pride as if they're protégé*
> *Then there's a sudden realisation*
> *at the end of the play*
> *That we're all a bit distracted*
> *by the choice of passageway!*
> *In 1599 was this really so risqué?*
> *Or simply an excuse to try on cute lingerie*
> *Or maybe Shaky fancied something*
> *more like Cabaret*
> *Girls will be Boys when they want*
> *their own way*
>
> *We've never had an issue*
> *Understanding young Viola*
> *She would have sold her brother for a life*
> *boat shaped gondola*
> *When she swapped her skirt for trousers*
> *She became the 'boy' men like*
> *The one that says he never would*
> *But looks as though he might!*

There was never a struggle
Understanding Portia
She dressed up as a lawyer
to get her way in court-A
A lofty attitude she showed
To poor Bassanio
She says her virtue's still intact
Though she like to go commando

CHORUS

Girls will be Boys when they want
their own way
Men take pride as if they're their protege
Then there's sudden realisation
at the end of the play
That we're all a bit distracted
by the choice of passageway!

It really doesn't matter
to us who you think you are
If you like a cigarillo
or a big cigar
The one thing we feel certain of
As Grandma always said
It's always come in handy
and has stood us in good stead
So if you hadn't realised
By now you should have guessed
That when it comes to being us....

They strip to their fabulous undies!

Breast is always best!

She has sharp teeth, within her mouth
Inside her dark red lips
And polish bright hides the sharpened claws
In her fingertips

> *And as she conceals her power*
> *All your strength is now on view*
> *You think you are possessing her*
> *But she has got her teeth in you*
> *In you*

There follows a big sexy dance break which is interrupted by MELCHIOR, dressed as Shakespeare.

MELCHIOR

Thank you, my Dears.

He stops the music and gestures for the girls to go to the back.

Saskia! Imogen!

His beloved children arrive on stage.

Ladies and Gentlemen. I have the privilege and honour to present to you, my family – my beloved Darling Buds of May and my muse and wife, Lady Atalanta Hazard!

As a finale, LADY ATALANTA appears dressed as Good Queen Bess. Shakespeare kisses her full on the mouth. The LUCKY CHANCES have faded into the background and have been returned to their rightful place in the CHORUS. What You Will is a huge success! On the final beat of the number, MELCHIOR turns into OLD MELCHIOR.

OLD MELCHIOR

Ladies and gentlemen, thank you very much, you have been a wonderful audience. And I'd now like to welcome to the stage the man who wrote, financed and conceived this evening's production, my dear twin brother Peregrine.

PEREGRINE is pushed on stage but he bashfully retreats back to the wings.

CHORUS

        Perry! Perry! Perry!

MELCHIOR

        I tried to persuade him to play the walk-on
        part of Falstaff but he prefers a life in the
        wings.

CHORUS

        Perry! Perry! Perry!

PEREGRINE is pushed on for a second time; he has turned into OLD
PEREGRINE.

OLD PEREGRINE

        For God's sake Melchior, enough of all
        that. Let's party.

We cut to behind the cloth where OLD PEREGRINE *pops champagne.*

OLD MELCHIOR

        Creatures of the theatre! A toast.

OLD PEREGRINE

        Champagne to all here, real pain to the
        other bastards!

ALL

        Real pain to the bastards!

SHOW DORA

        What a joy it is to dance and sing, Nora

SHOW NORA

        I'll drink to that, Dor.

The first night party continues as DORA *speaks to the audience.*

DORA

        Either the markets had recovered by this
        time, or a good deal of fiddling went on

while Rome was burning because me
and Nora had charge accounts opened
for us at Harrods by gents who kept it
from their wives.

*The LUCKY CHANCES pose provocatively in furs and laugh at
GRANDMA.*

GRANDMA

What the bloody hell have you got on?

SHOW DORA

Fur Grandma.

GRANDMA

What kind of fur?

**SHOW DORA
& SHOW NORA**

Fox.

GRANDMA

What are you thinking? You wouldn't
cut off a baby's head and stick it on your
best friend's flayed corpse for decoration,
would you?

SHOW NORA

I never met a fox socially, Grandma!

GRANDMA

Ooh La fucking la! Stars on your door,
stars in your eyes and stars exploding
where the common sense should be!

DORA

Sometimes we thought in our youthful
vanity that the old bag was jealous of
us. Now I am old, I think I know why
Grandma didn't like us at eighteen – we

70

felt no irony and how easily we were
impressed.

We are back at the first night party of 'What You Will'

OLD PEREGRINE

Half of the industry was in tonight. This
could be your big break, girls.

GRANDMA

Bottom's Up, Ducky!

OLD PEREGRINE

Just say the word, birdie!

> ***Sharp teeth when the world starts innin'***
> ***Sharp teeth when the girls start winnin'***
> ***Sharp teeth when the world starts grinnin'***
> ***Sharp teeth, make a little mischief.***
> ***Sharp teeth when the world starts spinnin'***
> ***Sharp teeth when the girls start winnin'***
> ***Sharp teeth, sharp teeth, sharp teeth,***
> ***make a little mischief.***

*The Girls are revolted by this flirting between GRANDMA and OLD
PEREGRINE and SHOW NORA and SHOW DORA work their way round
the party. Drinks flow and couples dance. OLD PEREGRINE comes and
scoops up the girls they do a brief dance routine together.*

OLD MELCHIOR

They are Peregrine's daughters you
know. He must be very proud.

*PEREGRINE and MELCHIOR start to argue. A waiter comes by with
oysters to eat.*

SHOW DORA

I don't fancy oysters, but have you got
anything else a girl could slip in?

71

The WAITER turns and it is the BLUE EYED BOY.

DORA

It was only my blue eyed boy.

SHOW DORA

Fancy meeting you here. I thought you had left

BLUE EYED BOY

Times are hard. Too many tenors, not enough songs.

SHOW NORA

Sharp teeth, sharp teeth, sharp teeth,
make a little mischief.

In the background NORA is standing on a table and singing a song.

BLUE EYED BOY

Nora…

SHOW DORA

I'm Nora. That's Dora. I'm here

SHOW DORA sings two verses from 'The Way You Look Tonight'. They kiss. And they kiss and kiss. They sink to the floor and make their way through the party until they are in MELCHIOR's dressing room. His cardboard crown sits there, pride of place.

SHOW DORA rips off her false eyelashes and reaches for the cold cream. She starts to take off her make-up.

BLUE EYED BOY

What are you doing Nora?

SHOW DORA

I want to be myself. I want to look like myself.

BLUE EYED BOY

You do look like yourself

SHOW DORA

No, I want it off. I want all of this shit off
of me

*She sings. The BLUE EYED BOY takes her hand and turns her round.
He picks up the cotton wool and wipes SHOW DORA's face for her. He
pours water out of the jug and rinses her face. She is wet now. He is
gentle and looks deeply into her eyes.*

BLUE EYED BOY

You're beautiful

SHOW DORA

I dye my hair.

BLUE EYED BOY

I know

SHOW DORA

I'm a natural mouse

BLUE EYED BOY

You're my mouse.

*He sings from 'The Way You Look Tonight'. They make tender simple
love and roll apart.*

Nora, you've changed your perfume

SHOW DORA sits up and looks straight at him.

DORA

I only had to speak to say 'Not Nora my
darling, but Dora. Dora, who loves you
and loves you only. I only had to speak
and there would have been one more
happy housewife behind some garden

73

fence in Slough or Cheam and a bellyful
of kids. Those words that would have
changed everything were on the very tip
of my tongue

*SHOW DORA, and the party guests, take an in-breath, but before she
can speak...*

BLUE EYED BOY

Can you smell burning?

PARTY GUESTS

FIRE!

*There is panic as everyone scrabbles for safety. The theatre is burning
down, the velvet curtains, the costumes, scenery.*

BLUE EYED BOY

Quick

SHOW DORA

I can't breathe

*The BLUE EYED BOY throws a towel over her head, to stop the smoke
and grabs a bunch of flowers from MELCHIOR's dressing table. He leads
her out of the burning palace.*

*SHOW DORA and the BLUE EYED BOY escape onto the street where
SHOW DORA buries her head in the BLUE EYED BOY's chest.*

BLUE EYED BOY

Nora. Precious Nora.

*The couple are showered with sparks and flame, a burning bride and
groom.*

SHOW DORA

Oh my God – my sister!

SHOW DORA pulls away from the tenor and begins her frantic search. More partygoers find their way out of the burning building but no sign of SHOW NORA.

> Nor! Nora! Where are you? I'm sorry. I'll give him up. I'll give it all up. I can't do this without you. I can't do anything without you. NORA!

In the chaos and smoke, SHOW DORA bumps into OLD MELCHIOR who is dragging his Shakespearean throne out of the flames.

OLD MELCHIOR

> Give us a hand

SHOW DORA helps him position his throne on the pavement.

> Champagne! Champagne! The theatre is destroyed!
> Dora? Or is it Nora? Come and take a glass of wine with the prince in exile dear child.

SHOW DORA

> I must say, you are taking this very well, sir.

OLD MELCHIOR

> Can't a man enjoy a glass of wine at his own fireside? The theatre is destroyed.

The WAITER pours MELCHIOR a drink.

> You've lost your eyebrows.

SHOW DORA

> *(Sobbing.)* Worse than that, I've lost my sister.

OLD MELCHIOR

> I've lost my crown. My foolish crown, my
> paper crown of a king of shreds and patches.
> The crown my father wore as Lear – to
> have survived so many deaths so much
> heartbreak, so many travels… Now, gone
> up in smoke. We mummers are such simple
> folk. Superstitious as little children. The
> fire was welcome to take anything, but that
> cardboard crown with the paint peeling off.
> It meant more to me than wealth, or fame,
> or women, or children. What shall I do
> without my crown?

He starts to cry. Tears streaming down his cheeks like chalk on a blackboard.

SHOW DORA starts to slow clap the performance. The surviving guests all look to the burning theatre and start to join the clap. Faster. Faster they go until…

OLD MELCHIOR

> *(Seeing PEREGRINE wearing his crown.)*
> My crown!

PARTYGOER 1

> Look!

PARTYGOER 2

> Clear the way!

PARTYGOER 1

> It's Peregrine

PARTYGOER 3

> It's a miracle

OLD PEREGRINE appears, enormous and heroic out of the flames. In his arms is SHOW NORA, on his head the cardboard crown, on her head a towel. He is ablaze with passion and adrenalin.

76

SHOW DORA starts towards SHOW NORA, but the BLUE EYED BOY runs right past her and pulls SHOW NORA from OLD PEREGRINE's arms. He laughs and cries and showers her with hugs and kisses.

SHOW NORA wakes but rather than kiss him back, says.

SHOW NORA

Where's Dora? Where's my sister?

BLUE EYED BOY

Oh, you brave girl. You went back to look for Dora. You risked your life.

SHOW NORA looks round and upon seeing SHOW DORA faints. A sister's discretion!

OLD MELCHIOR

My crown. Give me my crown! Give me the crown you bastard!

He whips off the crown and shakes it like a tambourine.

OLD PEREGRINE

If you want it, jump for it!

OLD MELCHIOR

My crown!

OLD PEREGRINE

Jump! The great genius, Melchior Hazard. Jump!

OLD MELCHIOR

My crown!

OLD PEREGRINE

Jump!

OLD MELCHIOR

My crown!

OLD PEREGRINE

> If you can't jump, then crawl in the dirt.

OLD PEREGRINE tosses the crown aside and OLD MELCHIOR scrabbles for it and holds it like a baby.

> You selfish shit.

OLD PEREGRINE takes off his coat and puts it round SHOW DORA's shoulders. He holds her face in his hands but she only has eyes for the BLUE EYED BOY.

> Time to go, Dora.

He gives her a cuddle.

> Time to take poor Nora home

SHOW NORA in the TENOR's arms takes a look at SHOW DORA. She knows what has happened.

OLD PEREGRINE, SHOW NORA and SHOW DORA hold on to each other.

DORA

> We gave the boy with eyes like sky a lift
> to Clapham Common but Uncle Perry
> wouldn't let him come all the way with
> us. I never saw him again.

SHOW DORA looks back at the man she will never have, the man who doesn't even know it is her that he has loved.

SCENE 2

We are back in Brixton. DORA and NORA are looking through photo albums and scrap books.

DORA

> Memory Lane is starting to wind in directions I don't like to remember, Nora. Is it time to get ready for the party yet? A bit of Crimson Lake always takes the edge off sadness.

NORA

> We've got to tell them about Grandma.

DORA

> I know. I do know.

NORA

> Grandma kept the programmes of every show we were ever in.

GRANDMA joins them from the past and takes over from NORA with the scrapbook.

> I feel bad when I see these scrapbooks, when I remember how we teased her

DORA

> How we'd bring home sausage rolls and crocodile handbags.

NORA

> But she would just keep on snipping out the cuttings and pasting them in.

DORA

> I remember once, haunts me it does, her coming into the bathroom with not a stitch on.

GRANDMA CHANCE slips off her coat and is naked. She goes into the bathroom.

>She never dreamt of knocking.

SHOW DORA is drying herself after a bath and both women are captured in front of the mirror, SHOW DORA is young and slim and trim and tender, GRANDMA is vast, sagging and quivering.

SHOW DORA giggles.

>I shouldn't have but I couldn't help it.
>And I could never take that giggle back.

GRANDMA

>That's all very well, Dora, but one fine
>day you'll wake up and find you're old
>and ugly, just like me.

DORA

>I'd never even thought that, years back,
>she might have been pretty. She went to
>get her dressing gown before she had a
>wee and there was a coolness after that
>lasted for months.

GRANDMA puts her coat back on and sits back down at the kitchen table, sticking the picture in the book, tip of her tongue between her teeth, all concentration.

NORA

>The last scrap book stops short in
>1944, leaving us marooned for ever just
>turning thirty…

GRANDMA dips it in the ink and writes underneath.

GRANDMA

>'Duke of York's Theatre. May 20th 1944'.

GRANDMA reaches for the stout but finds it empty.

Bugger.

She gets up and heads for the door. The air raid siren sounds but GRANDMA is undeterred.

DORA

No! Grandma!

NORA

Don't go out for more stout!

DORA

Stay here, safe and sound. Safe and loved, Grandma.

NORA

If you curb your thirst you'll live to see VE Day.

GRANDMA

(To DORA and NORA.) I'm not going to let Hitler inconvenience my drinking habits now, am I?

GRANDMA walks through the door. We hear the bombs fall and land.

NORA

And that was how we lost Grandma.

NORA, DORA, YOUNG DORA and YOUNG NORA and SHOW DORA and SHOW NORA sit in the house together. They feel its sudden emptiness. After a long, desolate pause.

SHOW NORA

Shall we go and find our Dad?

DORA

It is a characteristic of human beings that if they don't have a family of their own, they will invent one.

SHOW DORA

> Dad? No point. He still won't admit that
> he is anything to do with us.

SHOW NORA

> She does though. Lady Atalanta. Let's
> see if she fancies spicing up her stew
> with two more dumplings!

SHOW DORA

> Alright. Let's give it a try.

LADY ATALANTA appears.

LADY ATALANTA

> My dears! How wonderful to see you –
> you are both looking so well!

NORA

> I could feel my knees aching and chin
> sagging but she was polite if nothing else.

LADY ATALANTA

> There is so much for us to catch up on!
> Saskia and Imogen

DORA

> The darling Buds of May

LADY ATALANTA

> Are all grown up and have places at RADA!

NORA

> Or Ra di bloody Da as I like to call it!

LADY ATALANTA

> Melchior and I couldn't be prouder. Oh!
> It is so good to see you again, dear Dora
> and Nora!

They all embrace.

DORA

There was no love lost between us and the red headed horrors, so when Lady Atlanta invited us to their twenty-first birthday party...

LADY ATALANTA

You must come to the Bud's twenty-first Birthday party!

**SHOW NORA
& SHOW DORA**

Stuff that!

LADY ATALANTA

No, truly my dears. I want you both to be there. It's at our weekend cottage in Sussex so bring your wellies....

**SHOW DORA
and SHOW NORA**

Wellies?

LADY ATALANTA

Yes! It will be a real family affair. Melchior will be there, and Peregrine.

DORA and NORA

Our fathers...

SHOW DORA

Why is Peregrine coming? We haven't seen him for years.

LADY ATALANTA

He keeps in touch, dear man that he is. We used to be friends.

DORA

I do believe she twinkled a little!

NORA

> She did! That was definitely, positively a twinkle of the cheekiest order!

LADY ATALANTA

> See you at the party! Saskia and Imogen will be delighted to see you again.

SHOW NORA
and SHOW DORA

> I bet they will.

OLD PEREGRINE appears.

OLD PEREGRINE

> Girls

SHOW DORA
and SHOW NORA

> Uncle Perry!

OLD PEREGRINE

> Ready for the party?

SHOW NORA

> Only if you get us back to Brixton tonight.

OLD PEREGRINE

> Have you got everything?

SHOW NORA

> Not presents. Not for those vipers. I draw the line at birthday presents.

SHOW DORA

> I bought some flowers though. To show willing. I love a daffodil! Nothing beats a bit of spring!

84

OLD PEREGRINE

>Good girl, Dora. You wouldn't believe
>the flowers I have seen on my travels.

He pulls a flower out from his sleeve and gives it to SHOW DORA who puts it in her hair with a smile.

DORA

>Perry seemed bigger than ever and
>brown as a berry from the tropical sun.
>You'd never believe from the cut of his
>jib that he'd turned sixty.

OLD PEREGRINE

>Let's get going.

They get in to the car.

>Here we go.

They set off in PEREGRINE's Bentley convertible.

DORA

>He was distracted that day. All of
>a twitter, nervous, joyful, on edge,
>abstracted, all at once.

OLD PEREGRINE screams at the Gods, sighs then changes tack.

OLD PEREGRINE

>I'm going to give a lecture don'tcha
>know! At the Royal Society no less!
>'Butterflies of the World'. The creatures
>delight, inspire and move me, girls.
>And I've discovered new ones. Imagine
>that? I have held those papery triangles
>of colour and gazed at them before any
>other human has even heard of their
>existence. Imagine! I am going to devote
>the rest of my life to Lepidoptera.

He screams at the Gods again, only this time it is more of a wail.

NORA

> I knew in my water that there'd be tears before bedtime.

SHOW DORA
& DORA

> Hope for the best

SHOW DORA
& DORA

> Expect the worst

OLD PEREGRINE

> You go ahead, I'll follow.

SHOW DORA and SHOW NORA, knock on the farmhouse door carrying flowers. It is opened by two red headed horrors accompanied by their friend, a PRINKING MINX in a tutu.

SASKIA and IMOGEN

> Hello! Happy Birthday to us!

SASKIA

> *(Laughing at DORA's flowers and taking them.)*
> Daffodils! That's hilarious! "Which some call nature's bastards"! *Winter's Tale*, Act IV Scene III. How apt!

LADY ATALANTA

> My little Saskia is playing Perdita, she is quite obsessed, aren't you darling?

SASKIA

> If you say so, Ma.

LADY ATALANTA

> Welcome. The flowers are lovely! Everything is exquisite!

86

SHOW NORA snatches the flowers away from SASKIA and hands them kindly to LADY ATALANTA.

SHOW NORA

Exquisite indeed.

IMOGEN

We can't stay here talking to you, we have lines to learn for our party piece, don't we Saskia?

SASKIA

Yes we do… What was it? What was it? I have a brain like a sieve… Oh yes! I remember "Now God stand up for Bastards"! That's you two!

The BUDS giggle nastily.

PRINKING MINX

Hi girls.

SASKIA and IMOGEN

Hi.

PRINKING MINX

Let me show you some of my Martha Graham techniques.

SASKIA and IMOGEN

Oh. Do show! Do show. *(To DORA and NORA.)* We're at RADA together.

They dance as OLD MELCHIOR appears.

OLD MELCHIOR

Tell David Niven there's a reason he's not invited.

OLD MELCHIOR watches with approval as the young women contract and release. He looks handsome and dashing, even for sixty.

DORA and NORA
& SHOW DORA and NORA

>Pit a pat. Pit a pat.

OLD MELCHIOR

>Well! If it isn't my supporting cast and
>fellow thespians, The Lucky Chances!
>Come in, come in!

OLD MELCHIOR ushers SHOW NORA and SHOW DORA into the party.
He looks over his shoulder at the PRINKING MINX and gives her a
wink. She follows them in leaving IMOGEN and SASKIA outside with
OLD PEREGRINE.

SASKIA and IMOGEN

>Hallo, Uncle Perry

OLD PEREGRINE

>Pit a Pat. Pit a pat.

OLD PEREGRINE laughs and then cries.

SASKIA

>Come on in, Perry darling. You're
>behaving very strangely!

IMOGEN

>You look like you need a drink.

SASKIA

>And Dad needs his audience!

We all go in to the party.

OLD MELCHIOR

>*(To his assembled audience of party goers.)*
>Yes, Lear really is one of the last notches
>I needed on my theatrical cot. I hope
>you are able to understand what an
>honour this is for a humble old actor,

nearing the end of the greasepaint and
sawdust journey. We are all cast and go
into production next week – I hope I
can count on you all for the vital word
of mouth (the lifeblood of our humble
profession) and of course, for box office!

LADY ATALANTA

Come, come now, Melchior. We don't
need to be selling tickets now. This is the
girl's party. Today is all about them.

SASKIA

Be quiet Ma. We're fine! We love to hear
of Daddy's triumphs.

IMOGEN

We are so proud of you, Popsicle. So proud.

OLD PEREGRINE

Popsicle

SHOW DORA

You alright, Perry?

OLD PEREGRINE

Never better

He raises his glass.

To the girls!

ALL

To the girls

DORA

And then came the cake. Their cake,
from Harrods with twenty-one candles.

NORA

No cake in the world would be able to take
the number of candles we'd need now.

LADY ATALANTA holds the cake to her darling Buds and SASKIA and IMOGEN blow out the candles.

ALL

Wish! Wish! Wish!

The girls scrunch their eyes and wish for money, stardom and success.

OLD PEREGRINE

(Clearly moved.)
My Girls. My precious Girls

NORA

Of course, we'd always known deep
down inside that Perry was their father.

DORA

We tried to pretend otherwise and I was
jealous as hell of it but there you are.

Emotional, OLD PEREGRINE gathers SASKIA and IMOGEN to him. OLD MELCHIOR watches, unmoved.

OLD PEREGRINE

I can't tell you how much it means to
this old sinner to be among you all on
the day that you two precious copper
knobs finally reach your majorities, key
to the door, license to marry... but don't
rush off and marry too quickly, dearest
ones, and leave us all lonely.

It was tough, I can tell you to think of a
present fine enough for you two on this
day of days. Not baubles or bangles or
beads, but something that would last,
something as beautiful as you both that
would go on for ever. So...here you are.
With all my love.

He hands them each a diamond bracelet size box.

> Look what's inside my darlings!

The girls rip open the wrapping, open the boxes and scream. IMOGEN drops hers.

SASKIA

> Good God!

SASKIA and IMOGEN

> Caterpillars?

OLD PEREGRINE

> Soon to be butterflies. Named after you
> two! Saskia Hazard and Imogen Hazard.
> Two of the most beautiful butterflies in
> all the rainforest. As long as people love
> butterflies, your names will be on their lips,
> you'll have a kind of beautiful eternity.

IMOGEN

> Is that all?

She pokes it.

> I think mine's dead

SASKIA

> Thanks a lot. I hate it.

OLD PEREGRINE visibly crumples, deflates. He looks 110 years old.

OLD PEREGRINE

> Pit a pat. Pit a pat

OLD MELCHIOR steps in.

OLD MELCHIOR

> I too have prepared a very special
> surprise for my best, beloved
> daughters.... And one that I hope

will be a little more welcome, Perry!
I have for you, my treasures... a new....
beautiful....

DORA

Such timing. All eyes were upon him...

OLD MELCHIOR

Stepmother!

NORA

Oh! Now I was glad I was there alright!

LADY ATALANTA

What is this?

OLD MELCHIOR

(To LADY ATALANTA.) I'm sorry to do this
so publicly, my dear, but sometimes you
have to be cruel to be kind. And who can
resist a little drama when carried away
with life's romance! I have filed for divorce
and am going to marry my Cordelia!

LADY ATALANTA

Please. Stop it, Melchior, this isn't funny.

OLD MELCHIOR

No. This is not funny in the least. This is
passion, this is present, this is the beating
heart of life!

SASKIA

Your Cordelia?

LADY ATALANTA

No. No.

IMOGEN

Your Cordelia? But your Cordelia is...

92

LADY ATALANTA

Please don't do this to me…

SASKIA

My best friend!

OLD MELCHIOR holds his and out and the PRINKING MINX takes it – she is all Martha Graham and a slow curtsey!

OLD PEREGRINE

No fool like an old fool!

PRINKING MINX

I hope you don't mind girls? We wanted to surprise you on your birthday.

SASKIA

You scheming little bitch, I'll …

SASKIA lunges at the MINX.

LADY ATALANTA

Oh Saskia, Saskia. Don't make a scene. Please, this is too much.

IMOGEN and SASKIA attack the PRINKING MINX.

OLD MELCHIOR

(Slapping them hard.) Stop that, young ladies!

Both girls burst into tears.

MELCHIOR

(Shouts after them.)
Well, you spoilt little ingrates have made my final birthday gift a little easier to reveal… You are both cut off! Do you hear me? No more allowances! You can earn your own living now, like Peregrine and I have always done. Stand on your

own two feet for the first time in your
sheltered little lives.
(To the MINX.) Come along darling.
We are done here.

"Hell is empty and all the Devils are here". *The Tempest* **Act 1, Scene 2.**

Goodnight.

SASKIA

Fuck off, Daddy.

IMOGEN

Yes, just fuck off.

They storm off, each slamming the door behind them.

SHOW DORA

I'm going to call a bloody taxi

LADY ATALANTA

Oh, please don't go before coffee

OLD PEREGRINE

And I am going back to the jungle.
I look forward to the company of
crocodiles after being in the loving
bosom of my family.

He collapses onto the floor.

And yet I love them. God, I love them.
That's my punishment isn't it? My crime
is my punishment

DORA and NORA look down at their distressed, beloved uncle.

DORA

I'd never thought what it must be like to
be a father until that moment. Peregrine

> looked like the picture of Dorian Gray.
> The sky closed in, the sun disappeared
> and all was grey.

OLD PEREGRINE hugs SHOW NORA and SHOW DORA as if he would never let go.

> I think he loved Nora and myself as
> much as he loved Imogen and Saskia,
> if not more. But not, you understand in the
> same way. We were not flesh of his flesh.

OLD PEREGRINE leaves, a beaten man.

SHOW DORA

> I don't think we'll see him again.

SHOW NORA

> They should have made a go of it.

SHOW DORA

> Perry and Lady Atalanta?

SHOW NORA

> Perry and Grandma. He should have
> done the right thing and made a real
> family of us.

The phone rings.

SHOW DORA Answers it.

SHOW DORA
& SHOW NORA.

> 49 Bard Road.

SHOW DORA

> What? What! Slow down… Tell us what
> has happened.

SHOW NORA and SHOW DORA listen together like George and Mary in 'It's a Wonderful Life'.

Back in the farmhouse, seeing what is being described to NORA and DORA over the phone.

SASKIA and IMOGEN are crazed with rage and greed.

IMOGEN

We want what's ours.

SASKIA

Sign the papers.

IMOGEN

Yes, sign the papers, Mother.

LADY ATALANTA

Please, Girls. I'm not going to sign anything tonight. Everything will feel better in the morning.

SASKIA

But how will we live, Mother dearest? How will we live?

LADY ATALANTA

I will always take care of you.

IMOGEN

You didn't even stick up for us. No wonder daddy left you for a younger model.

LADY ATALANTA

Please girls, I don't deserve this.

SASKIA

Sign this. Sign this you pathetic old hag.

LADY ATALANTA

You're breaking my heart.

IMOGEN

And you're breaking our balls. Sign the
fucking papers.

SASKIA

If you loved us we wouldn't even have
to ask.

SASKIA cries.

LADY ATALANTA

Stop it.

LADY ATALANTA signs the papers.

SASKIA and IMOGEN

Thank you Mummy.

SASKIA

Right. Let's find the money.

The girls stuff as many valuables as they can grab into pillowcases.

LADY ATALANTA

Saskia, Imogen. Stay. Stay. We can have
tea and work things through.

*LADY ATALANTA tries to stop them but there is a kerfuffle and she falls
down the stairs.*

IMOGEN

Come on Saskia.

SASKIA

Let's get out of here.

They run down the stairs and out of the house.

DORA

She's so snagged her spine that she'd
never walk again.

NORA

Did she fall or was she pushed?

DORA

Not a word, nor whisper upon the
subject ever wormed its way through
Lady Atalanta's stiff upper lip.

NORA

But we do know that those dreadful girls
had just made her sign the Farm over to
them, plus all that remained of her last
bit of capital, before she took her tumble.

DORA

We couldn't help but be aware of that
because now she hadn't got a penny to
bless herself and nowhere to go either.

Into the phone.

SHOW DORA

Don't worry, we'll come over and get you.

DORA

And that was how we came to inherit the
Lady Atalanta

NORA

Though she's really no trouble.

*The two old ladies gently pick LADY ATALANTA up off the floor and
place her in her wheelchair.*

SCENE 3

We are back in the present.

NORA

> What shall we wear tonight? I've had
> enough of all this raking of old coals.
> We have a party to go to.

DORA

> There must be something upstairs we
> can wear. We've never thrown a stitch
> away and stowed all our old schmutter in
> Grandma's room.

The two women open the door on the room they have left untouched for years. The women start to take out dresses, clothes and memories and sit on the bed.

> Look at all this Nor.

NORA

> Half a century of evening wear. A history
> of the world in party frocks.

DORA

> We ought to donate it to the V&A.

NORA

> Why should someone pay good money to
> look at my old clothes?

DORA

> They used to pay good money to see you
> without them.

NORA

> They ought to put us into a museum.

DORA

> We ought to turn this house into a museum.

NORA

Museum of dust.

She finds the dress that DORA wore when she first made love with the blonde TENOR.

Look Dora! Remember this?

DORA

First kiss, first love, eyes as blue as sugar paper and skin like cream. I pray you, love, remember.

NORA

Here, Dora, nothing to cry about. What's going on?

DORA

Do you remember his name?

NORA

Whose name?

DORA

You gave me a present the day we were seventeen remember? Fifty-eight years ago today. It was my first time, remember?

NORA

I can only remember my first time, and the baby. Sometimes I feel a little lonely in the world. Don't you ever feel a little lonely too, Dora? No father, no mother, no chick nor darling child. Don't you ever want something to cuddle?

DORA

I have the cat when she wants to be fed

NORA

Sometimes it gets everso lonely with you
lost in the past while I'm left in 1989 with
old age

DORA

Don't talk like that about poor Lady Atalanta.

NORA

I don't mean wheelchair and well you
know it, I mean our old age. The fourth
guest at the table.

DORA

Look on the bright side, I've got you
and you've got me and we've both got
wheelchair our geriatric little girl. Our
real father might have reneged on the
job, but we had a loving dad in our Uncle
Perry. And we might have never known
our mother, but Grandma filled the gap
and you can say that again.

NORA

All the same, I wish.

DORA

No tears, Nor. No tears.
Let's get wheelchair ready for the party.

The women bath and dress WHEELCHAIR as if she were a treasured child.

> ***Mary made a pudding, nice and sweet,***
> ***Johnny took a knife and tasted it;***
> ***Taste, love, taste, love, don't say no.***
> ***Next Monday morning to the church***
> ***we will go.***

NORA

What are we going to wear?

The lights start to flicker.

I think Grandma's trying to tell us something.

DORA

She's telling us Memory Lane is a dead end.

GRANDMA pops out of the wardrobe.

GRANDMA

Come off it girls! Pluck the day! You ain't dead yet! You've got a party to go to! Expect the worst and hope for the best! Now get out there and buy yourselves some new clobber!

DORA and NORA

Toot Sweet Grandma, toot sweet!

With a flick of GRANDMA's hand, the house flies out from around them and, free from 49 Bard Road, they take to the streets of Brixton, walking tall and proud.

They walk past a vegetable stall. A young cheeky chap calls to them.

VEG MARKET MAN

Here, Gels! Fancy a widow's comfort?

He holds out an aubergine.

NORA

Is that the best you can do? I've seen bigger caterpillars turn into butterflies.

They walk past a man with leaflets and a placard.

DORA

Here, Nor, here come the animal rights.

ANIMAL RIGHTS MAN

Ere! That coat'd look better on a fox auntie.

NORA

It wouldn't look better on this fox, which
was humanely trapped in the Arctic Circle
by age old methods of an ecologically
sound Inuit hunter circa 1935, before
either you or your blessed mother, was
yet pissing on the floor, which trapper
has probably succumbed to alcohol and
despair due to having his traditional source
of livelihood taken away from him, and,
anyway, these foxes would be long dead,
by now, and rotted, if we weren't wearing
their lovingly preserved pelts.

NORA and CHORUS

Boom!

The ANIMAL RIGHTS MAN slopes off, defeated.

DORA

It's every woman's tragedy that, after a certain
age, she looks like a female impersonator.

NORA

What's every man's tragedy then?

DORA

That he doesn't.

*They are dolled up to the nines, make-up an inch thick and skirts; short
and tight.*

NORA

Do you think we've gone a little far?

DORA

The habit of applying war paint outlasts
the battle. Come on! We're not getting
any younger!

We fly to the bright side of the tracks
Side of the tracks.
Cut the London sky
Sharp as an Axe, sharp as an Axe

And with that, NORA, DORA and LADY ATALANTA in her wheelchair
take off and fly up into the air. They whoop with joy as they see London
below them.

Go to the east
Go to the west
Choose the one that you love best
Choose the one that you love best

We're crossing the river! The other
side of the tracks here we come. Old
father Thames lies between Brixton and
glamour like a sword

NORA

Look at the houses! All grand and white
and clean. Is that Sloane Square? Oh Dora,
there's his house!

DORA

Our father's house

They crash land outside MELCHIOR's house. An old drunk man is begging.
It is an ancient GORGEOUS GEORGE.

GORGEOUS GEORGE

I expected more but I'm satisfied.

DORA

'Ere, Nor. Is that who I think it is?

NORA

Bloody hell. It's only Gorgeous George.

DORA

George!

GORGEOUS GEORGE

Give us a bob.

DORA

He doesn't recognise us.

GORGEOUS GEORGE

Spare some change for an old comic…

DORA

You can have this on one condition. Spend it all on drink.

NORA and DORA spray themselves with Shalimar and Mitsouko and hold hands. They go into OLD MELCHIOR's party.

The company start to sing 'Is you is, or is you ain't, my baby?'

OLD MELCHIOR sits on a throne in a kaftan with jewelry and long pewter hair.

MELCHIOR sees DORA and NORA- and sees only them. He opens his arms.

OLD MELCHIOR

Dora! Nora! Now, my darlings. My darling daughters.

DORA and NORA gasp for air.

You must refresh my memory … which of you is it that uses Shalimar and which Mitsouko?

He smiles.

NORA starts to cry and OLD MELCHIOR stretches out his hand and touches her cheek.

OLD MELCHIOR

You shouldn't cry. Not at our birthday party. My darling daughters.

DORA starts to cry.

NORA and DORA

Dad.

OLD MELCHIOR opens his arms and the girls bury their heads, hearts and souls in his chest.

OLD MELCHIOR

My lovely and beloved daughters.

SASKIA

Dad! What are you saying? They're not your daughters. Stop it, Dad. It's embarrassing. Imogen come and help me sort this out.

IMOGEN

Enough Dad. That's enough!

OLD MELCHIOR

"But, hush! No more. Here are my chief guests."

SASKIA

How could you Daddy? How could you?

OLD MELCHIOR clasps DORA and NORA's hands.

IMOGEN

How could you choose them over us? How could you, Daddy?

DORA

Don't worry Darlin'.

NORA

She was egged on by the memory of
Goreous George on Brighton Pier.

DORA

'E's not your father!

DORA

(To the audience.) Comedy is tragedy that
happens to other people.

*Then, in on an almost magical wind, blow dozens of butterflies. They
land in NORA and DORA's hair. OLD PEREGRINE has arrived.*

OLD PEREGRINE

Happy Birthday, brother dearest.
And Happy Birthday my precious girls.
Noradora! You haven't changed a bit!
All our daughters. All our wonderful
daughters, Melchior. I've named a
butterfly for each one. Dora Chance

He blows a butterfly to the wind.

Nora Chance

He blows another one to the sky.

And I've even named this one for you,
you miserable old sod.

He blows a huge butterfly towards OLD MELCHIOR.

OLD PEREGRINE

(Turning to LADY ATALANTA.) Hi, there,
bright eyes. I should have named one for
you. Forgive me.
Ladies and Gentlemen, may I present
Lady Atalanta Hazard. The most
beautiful woman of her time.

SASKIA and IMOGEN

>Mother?

OLD MELCHIOR

>Attie?

SASKIA and IMOGEN

>Mother? We thought you were dead.

WHEELCHAIR/LADY ATALANTA grows with pride and recognition. She is beautiful.

OLD MELCHIOR

>Is that you? Bright eyes?

(PEREGRINE kisses LADY ATALANTA.)

>You and Peregrine? You didn't!

>How could you?

LADY ATALANTA takes the space.

LADY ATALANTA

>How could I? How could I? You
>hypocrite, Melchior. Do you not think
>that I was driven by the same passions
>and confusions as you? Do you not think
>that I had needs, that I had desires? You
>have no right to judge me, you who
>were profligate with your seed before
>me. You who seduced and abandoned
>an innocent girl, left her to die and then
>abandoned her motherless daughters?
>Your daughters! The daughters you
>never acknowledged until tonight – as if
>your Hazard blood might lose its virtue
>once mixed with that of a chambermaid.
>But please don't worry, it is still Hazard
>blood that made the Darling Buds of

May. They might have sprung from
Peregrine's seed and not your own, but
those girls are still cast in your mould!
They are the daughters that you loved
even when they robbed their mother of
her home and her money. They are the
daughters who spurned the love I gave
them just as you did yourself! But I am
still loved. I have found my family and it
is not a family of blood, it is a family of
choice. I am finally free and, thanks to
the love and care of these good women –
I am finally myself. My own true self.
Shame on you all.

SASKIA and IMOGEN cling to each other, a picture of shame and grief.

OLD PEREGRINE

It's true Melchior. They're mine, Melchior,
monsters that they are. Forgive me.
Forgive us all.

OLD MELCHIOR

You! You!

He buries his head in his hands.

SASKIA and IMOGEN go to their mother and hold the hem of her skirt.
She strokes their hair. OLD MELCHIOR is in distress.

Ay me! Poor soul is abandoned by all.

NORA

Not all, I've been here all the bloody
time.

OLD MELCHIOR

On the night of your seventeenth
birthday, I danced with Dora. Tonight,

with your permission, I will take the
floor with the other half of the apple.

MUSIC/UNDERSCORE

There may be trouble ahead,
But while there's moonlight and music
and love and romance,
Let's face the music and dance.

NORA and OLD MELCHIOR dance. SHOW NORA and YOUNG NORA
watch their older self. OLD PEREGRINE comes and joins DORA.

DORA

He's closed the circle

OLD PEREGRINE

God, Dora, I've been a cad.

DORA

You were always good to us, Perry.
Nora always said that you should have
married Grandma.

OLD PEREGRINE

What?!

DORA

Made a real family for us.

He guffaws and puts out his hand.

OLD PEREGRINE

How about it, Dora?

DORA

I don't fancy a foxtrot Perry, but I wouldn't
say no to a...

DORA kneels and puts her hands on OLD PEREGRINE's ankles. She
knows what she wants. OLD PEREGRINE falls to his knees and they take
each others' faces in their hands. They kiss passionately. As they make

love, they are surrounded by butterflies. NORA and OLD MELCHIOR
dance below. They are watched by YOUNG NORA and SHOW NORA.

OLD PEREGRINE and DORA lie back, spent.

OLD PEREGRINE

How long has it been, Dora?

DORA

Too long, me old cock!

OLD PEREGRINE laughs and starts to cough.

Whoa old sport! You don't want to peg it
on your 100th birthday!

OLD PEREGRINE

Don't care if I do!

DORA

I love you more than ever I loved any
young kid, short pants, mother doesn't
know he's out.

OLD PEREGRINE

Not bad for a centenarian, eh?

DORA

Not bad at all

YOUNG DORA and SHOW DORA enter and look at their old self.

SHOW DORA

But do not think that I went to bed that
night with a ribald ancient. Oh no.
I lay in the arms of that russet-mopped
young man in the checked trousers who'd
knocked at the door of 49 Bard Road
and saved us from gloom the day the war
to end all wars ended, just twenty years
before the next one started. And wars are

facts we cannot fuck away Perry, nor laugh
away either

Do you hear me Perry? No

That night, he was himself when young;
and also, when we were making love, he
turned into, of all people, that Blue-Eyed
Boy who'd never known my proper
name. That night was a kaleidoscope of
faces, gestures, caresses. He was not the
love of my life but all the loves of my life
at once.

YOUNG PEREGRINE comes and joins OLD PEREGRINE.

YOUNG DORA

And who was I? I saw myself reflected in
those bracken eyes of his. I was a skinny
girl with a green bow in her mouse
hair, blinking away from the first, worst
disappointment of her life in the sun on
Brighton Prom.

She gasps as a memory returns to her.

When I was thirteen years old. Oh Perry.
How could you?

GRANDMA CHANCE appears. She is horrified.

GRANDMA

Perry!

ALL

Perry!

SHOW DORA

You dirty beast.

CHORUS

(Singing.) She has sharp teeth within her mouth,
Inside her dark red lips,
And polish bright hides the sharpened claws
In her finger tips.

And when the game turns into war,
He takes out his long knife –
Concealing what he meant it for,
Which is, to take her precious life

DORA

You did me wrong, Perry. And no toy theatres, ice creams or dancing lessons can ever make it right.

OLD PEREGRINE

Forgive me, Dora.

DORA

Forgive you? You stole my childhood, Peregrine.

She pulls herself together.

But it doesn't matter now. Nothing matters. We'll never be wise children and I don't give a monkey's anymore.

OLD PEREGRINE

Tread carefully, Dora. Truth is a slippery creature. Look away and it plays tricks on you.

DORA

Truth is truth Peregrine. And I am not looking away. I see you. I see you more clearly than I ever have before. Oh,

and if we're talking slippery creatures,
you might take a moment to look in the
mirror.

DORA sits proudly on MELCHIOR's throne. GRANDMA CHANCE picks up MELCHIOR's crown and puts it on DORA's head. For a moment she is the legitimate Queen of all that is true and all that is resilient.

Ow! Something's not right. Something's
digging into my head.

She feels MELCHIOR's crown of cardboard perched on her head.

I've never been one for crowns of any sort.

She takes it off.

OLD PEREGRINE

My father's cardboard crown. You should
return it to its rightful owner

DORA

Perhaps we will.

DORA and NORA go to OLD MELCHIOR.

Father, look what I've found.

DORA and NORA place the crown on their father's head.

OLD MELCHIOR

Crowned, by my two dancing princesses.
My crown. My precious crown.

NORA

Just what he always wanted. Eh, Dor?

DORA

(To PEREGRINE and MELCHIOR.) Are you
two still here?

OLD PEREGRINE and OLD MELCHIOR exit along with their younger selves.

DORA

>And then a very strange thing happened, a very wonderful thing.

There is a knock at the door.

GRANDMA

>Get the door Noradora. I'm not getting any younger.

YOUNG NORA and YOUNG DORA go to the door. There are two babies on the doorstep with a note attached. They pick up the babies and hand the note to GRANDMA CHANCE.

>*(Reading.)* "Please look after my babies. No man, no money and no hope."

DORA

>Poor desperate wretch. Some things never change.

GRANDMA

>Two small mites in need of someone to love 'em!

YOUNG DORA and YOUNG NORA give the babies to NORA.

NORA

>Babies! Just what I always wanted! But I can't keep 'em. I'm seventy-five today.

DORA

>Grandma was fifty if she was a day when she took us in.

NORA

>And she didn't care who we were or where we came from.

DORA

I asked her once where she came from herself and she said

GRANDMA

Out of a bottle like a genie, Dearie

NORA

But I'm not their mother. And I'm not their father.

NORA

But I'm not their mother. And I'm not their father

DORA

'Father' is a hypothesis but 'Mother' is fact. Mother is as mother does.

EPILOGUE

NORA

I thought I might clear out Grandma's old room for a nursery, get rid of all that junk. Get a bloke to paint it white, with maybe a Beatrix Potter frieze. What do you think?

DORA

We won't be able to go out in the evening, Nora.

NORA

You can go out, dear. I'll be perfectly content to stay at home with these little cherubs.

DORA

No fun going out without you

NORA

        Come off it, Dora. Grow up.

DORA

        It's all very well for you Nora. You always
        wanted kids. Now you've got them

NORA

        We're both of us mothers and both of us
        fathers. They'll be wise children alright.

DORA

        'Ere, Nora ... if we've got these twins to
        look out for, we can't afford to die for at
        least another twenty years!

They laugh and the babies mew and rustle.

        What's up, small fry?

NORA

        I say, Dora, let's give them a song.

They sing 'Oh, girls just wanna have fun...'

**ALL THE DORA'S
and NORA'S**

        What a joy it is to dance and sing!

fun...

THE END.